C000136961

BRITTANY TRAVEL GUIDE 2023

By James Bartlett

Copyrighted Material © 1

All rights reserved.No part of this publication may be reproduced, distributed, or transmitted in any form in any way from or by any means, including photocopying, recording, or other electronic or mechanical methods, without prior written permission of the publisher, except in the case of brief quotations embodied in critical reviews and certain other noncommercial uses permitted by copyright laws.
Copyright © James Bartlett,2023

Table of Content

Copyrighted Material © 3

Copyrighted Material © 4

1. Introduction

As a seasoned travel expert, I recently embarked on an unforgettable journey to the enchanting region of Brittany in France. From the moment I arrived, I was captivated by its unique blend of history, breathtaking landscapes, and vibrant culture. I'd like to share with you a personal experience.

My adventure began in the picturesque town of Saint-Malo, renowned for its fortified walls and rich maritime heritage. As I strolled through the cobblestone streets, the salty breeze of the Atlantic Ocean filled the air, instantly transporting me back in time. The magnificent views of the coastline from the top of the ramparts left me awestruck, reminding me of the region's past as a Corsair stronghold.

Copyrighted Material © 5

Next, I made my way to the stunning Mont Saint-Michel, an iconic island abbey that seemed straight out of a fairy tale. Walking across the causeway towards the abbey, I marveled at its medieval architecture and the interplay between the shifting tides and the surrounding marshes. Exploring the narrow alleys and climbing to the abbey's pinnacle rewarded me with breathtaking panoramic views of the surrounding countryside.

Continuing my journey, I ventured inland to discover the mystical wonders of the Brocéliande Forest. This legendary forest, steeped in Arthurian tales, stirred my imagination. As I hiked through the lush greenery and ancient oaks, I couldn't help but feel a sense of magic in the air. I stumbled upon the mythical Fountain of Barenton, its crystal-clear waters inviting me to take a moment of tranquility and

Copyrighted Material © 6

reflect on the legends that unfolded within these woods.

The rugged coastline of the Pink Granite Coast beckoned me next, with its striking rock formations sculpted by the relentless waves. I embarked on a scenic coastal hike, marveling at the pink-hued boulders contrasting with the azure waters of the Atlantic. The unique geological formations, such as the famous "Sentinels of Ploumanac'h," created a surreal landscape that left me in awe of nature's artistry.

No visit to Brittany would be complete without indulging in its culinary delights. I treated myself to mouthwatering crêpes and galettes, savoring the traditional flavors of the region. The aroma of freshly caught seafood filled the air in the charming fishing village of Cancale, where I delighted in a feast of succulent oysters. Each bite was a symphony of flavors, a

Copyrighted Material © 7

testament to Brittany's reputation as a gastronomic paradise.

As I traveled further south, I encountered the vibrant city of Rennes, the capital of Brittany. The city's historic center, with its half-timbered houses and bustling squares, exuded a lively atmosphere. I immersed myself in the local culture, exploring the vibrant markets, admiring the stunning Saint-Pierre Cathedral, and savoring regional specialties in quaint bistros. Rennes' youthful energy, thanks to its large student population, added a dynamic flair to the city's already charming ambiance.

To conclude my journey, I ventured to the mystical Carnac, home to one of the most extensive megalithic sites in the world. Walking among the ancient standing stones, I couldn't help but marvel at the mysteries surrounding their origin. The alignment of these imposing monoliths seemed to connect the past and present,

Copyrighted Material © 8

evoking a sense of wonder and curiosity within me.

As I bid farewell to Brittany, I carried with me cherished memories of its breathtaking landscapes, rich history, and warm-hearted people. The region's unique blend of natural beauty, cultural heritage, and culinary delights left an indelible mark on my soul. Brittany truly captured my heart and ignited a desire to explore more of the world's hidden gems.

A. Welcome to Brittany

Welcome to the charming region of Brittany, located in the northwest corner of France. With its rich history, stunning landscapes, and unique cultural heritage, Brittany offers a captivating experience for travelers. This comprehensive guide aims to assist you in exploring the region's

Copyrighted Material © 9

highlights, providing valuable information and tips to make your journey truly unforgettable.

B. How to Use this Guide

To make the most of this guide, we recommend following these steps:

> ➤ Familiarize Yourself with Brittany: Begin by acquainting yourself with a general overview of Brittany, including its geographical location, climate, and cultural significance. Understanding the region's background will help you appreciate its distinct character.

> ➤ Plan Your Itinerary: Brittany has a diverse range of attractions, from historic sites to picturesque coastal towns, stunning landscapes to lively

festivals. Determine your interests and priorities, and use the provided information to plan an itinerary that suits your preferences.

➢ Getting There and Around: Learn about the transportation options available to reach Brittany, including international flights, train services, and road networks. Once you've arrived, explore the various methods of transportation within the region, such as trains, buses, and rental cars.

➢ Accommodation: Discover the different types of accommodation available in Brittany, from luxury hotels to budget-friendly guesthouses. Consider your budget, location preferences, and desired amenities when choosing the perfect place to stay.

Copyrighted Material © 11

➢ Cultural Etiquette: Familiarize yourself with the local customs and etiquette to ensure a respectful and enjoyable experience. Learn about greetings, dining etiquette, and social norms to interact with the locals politely.

➢ Brittany's Top Attractions: Delve into the highlights of Brittany, including its iconic landmarks, historical sites, natural wonders, and cultural events. Each attraction is described in detail, providing historical context, practical information, and insider tips.

➢ Outdoor Activities: Brittany's diverse landscapes offer ample opportunities for outdoor enthusiasts. Discover the region's hiking trails, coastal walks, water sports, and cycling routes. Whether you prefer an adrenaline-fueled adventure or a

Copyrighted Material © 12

leisurely exploration, Brittany has something for everyone.

➤ Culinary Delights: Brittany is renowned for its delectable cuisine, showcasing fresh seafood, savory crepes, and delicious pastries. Explore the region's culinary specialties, traditional dishes, and recommended restaurants. Don't forget to pair your meals with local beverages, including cider and Breton whisky.

➤ Shopping and Souvenirs: Uncover the vibrant shopping scene in Brittany, from bustling markets to charming boutiques. Learn about unique local products, such as artisanal crafts, locally produced food items, and distinctive clothing. Find the perfect souvenir to commemorate your trip. To remember your vacation, find the ideal memento.

Copyrighted Material © 13

➢ Practical Information: This section covers essential information, such as currency exchange, emergency contacts, healthcare facilities, and safety tips. Familiarize yourself with these details to ensure a smooth and hassle-free journey.

As you embark on your journey through Brittany, we hope this expert guide proves to be an invaluable resource. By following its recommendations and taking advantage of the provided insights, you'll be well-equipped to explore the region's wonders, immerse yourself in its rich culture, and create lasting memories. Enjoy your time in Brittany and savor the unique experiences that await you. Bon voyage!

Copyrighted Material © 14

11. Getting to Know Brittany

Renowned for its rich cultural heritage, breathtaking landscapes, and unique climate, Brittany offers a truly enchanting experience for travelers. Whether you're seeking picturesque coastal vistas, lush green countryside, or fascinating historical sites, Brittany has it all.

A. Geography & Climate

In this comprehensive guide, we will delve into the geography and climate of Brittany, providing you with essential insights to make the most of your journey. Join us as we embark on an extraordinary exploration of this remarkable region.

Location & Overview

Copyrighted Material ©

Situated in the northwestern part of France, Brittany occupies a peninsula jutting out into the Atlantic Ocean. Bordered by the English Channel to the north and the Bay of Biscay to the south, this geographically diverse region spans over 27,000 square kilometers (10,400 square miles). Brittany is divided into four departments: Finistère, Côtes-d'Armor, Morbihan, and Ille-et-Vilaine.

The landscape of Brittany is characterized by a harmonious blend of dramatic coastline, idyllic beaches, rolling hills, and verdant valleys. Its strategic location has shaped Brittany's history and culture, creating a unique fusion of Celtic, Gallic, and French influences. From charming fishing villages to medieval towns, every corner of this region tells a captivating story.

Coastal Beauty

Brittany boasts a coastline that stretches over 2,700 kilometers (1,700 miles), offering a mesmerizing tapestry of cliffs, sandy beaches, and picturesque islands. The rugged beauty of the Pink Granite Coast in Côtes-d'Armor showcases fascinating rock formations sculpted by the relentless ocean waves. As you wander along the coastal trails, you'll be captivated by the stunning interplay of light and shadow on the pink-hued rocks.

Further south, the Gulf of Morbihan beckons with its calm waters and sheltered islands. This natural harbor, often referred to as the "Little Sea," is a haven for sailors, kayakers, and nature enthusiasts. Explore the enchanting islands scattered across the gulf, each with its distinct character and charm. Don't miss the opportunity to visit Île-aux-Moines, known for its unspoiled beauty and peaceful atmosphere.

Copyrighted Material © 17

For a truly magical experience, head to the Crozon Peninsula in Finistère. This rugged and untamed stretch of coastline boasts towering cliffs, hidden coves, and pristine beaches. Marvel at the majestic beauty of Cap de la Chèvre, offering panoramic views of the Atlantic Ocean. Nature lovers will also appreciate the Parc Naturel Régional d'Armorique, a protected area encompassing diverse ecosystems and unique wildlife.

Countryside & Inland Delights

While the coastline steals the spotlight, Brittany's inland regions offer a wealth of natural beauty and cultural treasures. The Armorican Massif, a sprawling mountain range, covers a significant portion of the region. Its gentle slopes, covered in heather and gorse, provide a picturesque backdrop for hikers and nature enthusiasts. Explore the legendary Forest of Brocéliande in

Copyrighted Material © 18

Ille-et-Vilaine, an ancient woodland steeped in Arthurian legends and mythical tales.

Brittany is also home to numerous charming villages and towns that exude a distinct sense of history and tradition. Quimper, the cultural capital of Brittany, enchants visitors with its well-preserved medieval center and iconic cathedral. Wander through its narrow streets, lined with half-timbered houses adorned with colorful flowers. In Morbihan, discover the captivating town of Vannes, known for its well-preserved medieval ramparts and the stunning Château de Josselin.

The rural heartland of Brittany offers a patchwork of fields, orchards, and meandering rivers. The Nantes-Brest Canal, a tranquil waterway that winds through the countryside, presents an opportunity for leisurely boat rides or scenic walks along its towpaths. Explore the charming village of Rochefort-en-Terre, voted one of the most

Copyrighted Material © 19

beautiful villages in France, with its quaint medieval architecture and vibrant floral displays.

Climate & Weather

Brittany enjoys a mild oceanic climate, influenced by the Atlantic Ocean. The region experiences moderate temperatures throughout the year, making it an appealing destination for outdoor activities and exploration. The climate is characterized by mild summers and cool winters, with rainfall evenly distributed throughout the year.

★ Summer (June to August) brings pleasant temperatures, averaging around 20-25°C (68-77°F). It is the ideal time to enjoy Brittany's stunning beaches and coastal activities. The sea temperature is also at its warmest during this period, inviting swimmers and water sports enthusiasts.

Copyrighted Material © 20

★ Autumn (September to November) paints the landscape in vibrant hues, offering a picturesque backdrop for countryside walks and exploration. The temperatures gradually cool down, ranging from 15-20°C (59-68°F), and rainfall increases slightly.

★ Winter (December to February) in Brittany is generally mild, with temperatures averaging around 5-10°C (41-50°F). It is a quieter season, providing an opportunity to immerse yourself in the region's cultural heritage and indulge in hearty Breton cuisine. Some areas may experience occasional frost or snow, particularly in higher elevations.

★ Spring (March to May) breathes new life into Brittany, as nature awakens with blossoming flowers and lush

Copyrighted Material ©

green landscapes. Temperatures gradually rise, ranging from 10-15°C (50-59°F). Spring is an excellent time to explore Brittany's gardens, visit charming villages, and embark on hiking or cycling adventures.

It's worth noting that Brittany's coastal areas can experience strong winds, particularly during the winter months. These winds, known as the "Breton winds," contribute to the region's distinctive climate and are cherished by sailors and windsurfers seeking thrilling adventures.

As you venture into the captivating region of Brittany, its diverse geography and unique climate will continually captivate you. From the rugged beauty of its coastal landscapes to the tranquil charm of its countryside, Brittany offers an array of experiences for adventurous travelers. Embrace the mild climate and immerse yourself in the region's rich cultural heritage. Whether you're

Copyrighted Material © 22

seeking coastal exploration, historical wonders, or scenic countryside retreats, Brittany promises to be a destination that will leave an indelible mark on your heart. Embark on your journey and unlock the enchanting secrets of this extraordinary region.

B. History, Culture & The Present

With a rich tapestry of history, vibrant culture, and breathtaking landscapes, Brittany offers a truly immersive experience for travelers seeking an authentic and unforgettable adventure. This guide will take you on a journey through the detailed history, culture, and present-day allure of Brittany, providing you with essential insights to make the most of your visit.

A Tapestry of History

Ancient Roots & Celtic Heritage

★ Prehistoric Era: Brittany's history dates back thousands of years, evidenced by the awe-inspiring prehistoric sites such as the Carnac Megaliths, where rows of ancient standing stones are shrouded in mystery.

★ Celtic Influence: The region's Celtic roots run deep, with tribes like the Veneti establishing a significant presence in the area, leaving behind remarkable artifacts and legends that still resonate today.

Breton Identity & Medieval Splendor

★ The Breton Kingdom: In the 9th century, Brittany emerged as an independent kingdom, fostering a distinct Breton identity that persists to this day.

Copyrighted Material ©

★ Impressive Fortresses: Medieval fortresses like the Château de Fougères and the Fort National in Saint-Malo stand as testaments to Brittany's strategic importance and turbulent history.

Maritime Power & Exploration

★ Corsairs and Privateers: During the Age of Sail, Breton ports like Saint-Malo flourished as bases for corsairs and privateers, who ventured forth to challenge rival powers and engage in lucrative maritime activities.

★ Jacques Cartier: Born in Saint-Malo, Jacques Cartier made his mark as an intrepid explorer, credited with discovering Canada and laying the foundations for French colonization.

Resistance & Remembrance

Copyrighted Material © 25

★ Breton Resistance: In World War II, Brittany played a pivotal role in the French Resistance, bravely resisting German occupation and harboring escape networks for Allied soldiers.

★ Historic Sites: The Mont Saint-Michel, a UNESCO World Heritage site, served as a refuge during the war, while the haunting Memorial de la Shoah in Rennes stands as a somber reminder of the Holocaust.

Cultural Enchantment

Breton Language & Traditions

★ Breton Language: Breton, a Celtic language, is still spoken by a portion of the population, reflecting the region's linguistic heritage and cultural pride.

★ Festivals and Festivities: Brittany's calendar is brimming with vibrant festivals like the Festival Interceltique de Lorient, where musicians, dancers, and artisans celebrate Celtic traditions.

Gastronomy & Culinary Delights

★ Seafood Extravaganza: Brittany's extensive coastline blesses the region with an abundance of fresh seafood, such as oysters from Cancale and succulent lobster from the Armor Coast.

★ Crêpes and Cider: Indulge in traditional Breton cuisine with savory buckwheat crêpes, accompanied by a glass of locally produced cider—a true culinary delight.

Artistic Expression & Breton Pride

Copyrighted Material © 27

★ Traditional Crafts: Brittany's artistic heritage shines through its traditional crafts, including intricate lacework from Pont-l'Abbé and colorful pottery from Quimper.

★ Breton Music and Dance: The region's vibrant music scene features traditional instruments like the bombarde and accordion, complementing lively Breton dances like the famous "An Dro."

Enchanting Landscapes & Legends

★ Coastal Wonders: Brittany boasts a breathtaking coastline dotted with dramatic cliffs, pristine beaches, and charming fishing villages, including the enchanting Belle-Île and the captivating Pink Granite Coast.

★ Mystical Forests: Delve into the mystical depths of Brocéliande Forest,

Copyrighted Material © 28

steeped in Arthurian legends and home to ancient trees like the legendary Merlin's Oak.

★ Megalithic Marvels: Explore the intriguing alignment of Carnac's megalithic stones, an archaeological wonder that sparks the imagination and invites contemplation.

Present-Day Charm

Coastal Retreats & Quaint Towns

★ Saint-Malo: Immerse yourself in the historic charm of Saint-Malo, with its imposing ramparts, picturesque streets, and stunning views of the English Channel.

★ Quimper: Experience the beauty of Quimper, a town renowned for its medieval architecture, vibrant

Copyrighted Material © 29

markets, and the impressive Cathedral of Saint-Corentin.

Nautical Adventures & Watersports

★ Sailing and Boating: Embrace Brittany's maritime heritage by embarking on a sailing adventure, navigating its scenic waterways, or indulging in a boat trip to discover hidden coves and islands.

★ Surfing and Windsurfing: With its powerful Atlantic waves, Brittany's coast is a paradise for surfers and windsurfing enthusiasts, offering thrilling experiences and stunning coastal vistas.

Outdoor Exploration & Nature's Splendor

★ GR34 Coastal Path: Lace up your hiking boots and embark on the GR34, a legendary coastal path that winds its

Copyrighted Material © 30

way along Brittany's shoreline, treating you to breathtaking views and unspoiled nature.

★ Natural Parks: Discover the pristine beauty of the Parc Naturel Régional d'Armorique and the Parc Naturel Régional de Brière, home to diverse ecosystems, rare wildlife, and tranquil landscapes.

Cosmopolitan Delights & Cultural Centers

★ Rennes: Explore the vibrant capital city of Rennes, a bustling hub of culture, art, and history, boasting a lively student population and a vibrant gastronomic scene.

★ Nantes: Just outside Brittany's borders, Nantes offers a captivating blend of historic charm and contemporary innovation, with attractions like the Château des Ducs

Copyrighted Material © 31

de Bretagne and the iconic mechanical elephant.

As you embark on your journey through Brittany, you will be captivated by the region's intricate history, rich cultural tapestry, and enchanting blend of ancient traditions and modern allure. From its ancient megaliths to its medieval fortresses, from its lively festivals to its tantalizing cuisine, and from its breathtaking landscapes to its vibrant cities, Brittany promises a truly immersive and unforgettable experience. Whether you seek to unravel the mysteries of the past, indulge in the cultural treasures of the present, or find solace in the embrace of nature, Brittany invites you to embark on a journey that will leave an indelible mark on your heart and soul. So pack your bags, set forth on an adventure, and let the magic of Brittany unfold before your eyes.

Copyrighted Material © 32

C. Language & Etiquette

As you embark on your journey through this enchanting land, it's essential to familiarize yourself with the language and etiquette of Brittany. In this comprehensive guide, we will delve into the nuances of Breton, the region's traditional language, and provide insights into the local customs and manners that will help you navigate and immerse yourself in the unique culture of Brittany.

Part 1: Breton Language

Historical Context

Breton, or Brezhoneg, is a Celtic language spoken primarily in Brittany. It belongs to the Brythonic branch of the Celtic language family, which includes Welsh and Cornish. The origins of Breton can be traced back to the migrations of Celtic peoples across Europe. While the language's usage has

Copyrighted Material © 33

declined over the years, concerted efforts have been made to preserve and revitalize it.

Language Resources

While many locals in Brittany speak French, particularly in urban areas, a basic understanding of Breton can be a valuable asset during your travels. Consider utilizing the following resources to learn more about the language:

★ Language Apps: There are several smartphone applications available that offer Breton language lessons, vocabulary, and pronunciation guides.

★ Language Classes: Look for language classes or workshops in Brittany that cater to tourists interested in learning Breton. c.

★ Phrasebooks: Carry a pocket-sized Breton phrasebook to assist you in

Copyrighted Material © 34

basic conversations and help bridge any language gaps.

Language Etiquette

When engaging with Breton speakers, keep these language etiquette tips in mind:

★ Greetings: It is customary to greet others with a warm "Demat" (hello) when entering a shop, restaurant, or any public space. Using a few basic Breton phrases will be appreciated and demonstrate your interest in the local culture.

★ Pronunciation: Breton has some unique phonetic sounds. Take time to practice the pronunciation of words and names, showing respect for the language and its speakers.

★ Politeness: Demonstrating politeness by using phrases like "Mar plij" (please) and "Trugarez" (thank you) will help create a positive impression and foster goodwill.

Part 2: Etiquette & Customs

Greetings & Social Etiquette

★ Handshakes: When meeting someone for the first time, a firm handshake is the most common form of greeting.

★ Kisses on Cheeks: In informal settings, it is customary to exchange kisses on the cheeks. The number of kisses may vary depending on the region, but two kisses are generally common.

★ Punctuality: Being punctual is valued in Brittany. Arriving a few minutes early for social engagements or appointments is considered respectful.

Dining Etiquette

★ Table Manners: Keep your elbows off the table and wait for the host or hostess to start eating before you begin. It is also customary to say "Bon appétit" before you start your meal.

★ Bread Etiquette: Bread is an essential part of French cuisine, and in Brittany, it holds great importance. Break your bread instead of cutting it with a knife, and never put bread directly on your plate.

★ Cheese Course: Cheese is often served before or after the main course. Take small portions and enjoy it with bread, but avoid cutting the cheese in advance.

★ Wine Etiquette: Wine is commonly enjoyed with meals in Brittany. Wait for the host to offer a toast before taking your first sip, and remember to

Copyrighted Material ©

keep your glass below halfway full to indicate that you would like more.

Dress Code & Appearance

★ Casual Elegance: Brittany has a relaxed and casual atmosphere, but it is appreciated when visitors dress neatly and avoid overly casual or revealing attire in formal or religious settings.

★ Beachwear: When visiting coastal areas, it is acceptable to wear beachwear and swimsuits on the beach but cover up when entering shops, restaurants, or public places.

★ Formal Occasions: If you're attending formal events or dining at upscale establishments, it is customary to dress in elegant attire, such as dresses or suits.

Cultural Sensitivity

★ Religious Sites: When visiting churches or religious sites, dress modestly and avoid loud conversations or disruptive behavior to show respect for the sacred space.

★ Language Use: While French is widely spoken in Brittany, making an effort to learn a few Breton phrases is appreciated. However, avoid using Breton in situations where the other person may not understand it, as it may create confusion or misunderstandings.

★ Photography Etiquette: Always ask for permission before taking photographs of individuals, particularly in intimate or sacred spaces. Be mindful of local customs and traditions regarding photography.

Copyrighted Material ©

By understanding the language and etiquette of Brittany, you will not only enhance your travel experience but also show respect for the local culture. Embrace the warmth and hospitality of the Breton people as you immerse yourself in this captivating region of France.

D. Festivals & Events

While exploring this picturesque region, one cannot miss the opportunity to immerse oneself in the vibrant festivals and events that define the essence of Brittany's unique identity. From traditional celebrations to contemporary gatherings, Brittany offers a plethora of experiences that cater to diverse interests and leave a lasting impression on every traveler. In this guide, we will unveil the enchanting world of Brittany's festivals and events, providing you with an insider's perspective on how to make the most of your visit to this captivating region.

Copyrighted Material © 40

The Festival Interceltique de Lorient

Spanning ten days in August, the Festival Interceltique de Lorient in Lorient is a celebration of Celtic cultures from around the world. With over 700,000 visitors each year, this festival offers a mesmerizing experience of music, dance, art, and gastronomy. Immerse yourself in the rhythms of traditional Celtic music, witness vibrant parades showcasing diverse Celtic nations, and indulge in delicious culinary delights. From the Bagadoù (traditional Celtic bands) competition to the mesmerizing Grand Parade, this festival is an unmissable highlight for anyone interested in Celtic culture.

La Fête des Remparts de Dinan

Step back in time to the medieval era at the Fête des Remparts in Dinan, a town steeped in history and charm. Held every two years

Copyrighted Material © 41

in July, this festival brings the medieval heritage of Dinan to life. Witness knights in shining armor, jousting tournaments, traditional crafts, and captivating street performances. The town's cobbled streets and ancient ramparts serve as a perfect backdrop for this immersive experience, transporting visitors to a bygone era.

Festival de Cornouaille

For a true taste of Breton traditions, head to Quimper in July for the Festival de Cornouaille. Celebrating the cultural richness of the Cornouaille region, this festival showcases Breton music, dance, language, and folklore. Marvel at the spectacle of bagad bands, admire the intricate costumes of traditional dancers and savor the flavors of authentic Breton cuisine. The Festival de Cornouaille provides an immersive experience that celebrates the deep-rooted cultural heritage of Brittany.

Copyrighted Material © 42

Les Filets Bleus in Concarneau

Taking place in the enchanting coastal town of Concarneau, Les Filets Bleus is a lively festival that commemorates the town's fishing traditions. Held annually in August, this event features colorful parades, traditional Breton music, dance performances, and an array of seafood delicacies. Immerse yourself in the maritime atmosphere as the town comes alive with maritime-themed activities and celebrate the enduring connection between Concarneau and its fishing heritage.

Festival des Vieilles Charrues

Every July, the small village of Carhaix-Plouguer transforms into a musical hub, hosting one of France's largest music festivals: the Festival des Vieilles Charrues. Drawing renowned international artists and a vibrant crowd of music enthusiasts, this

Copyrighted Material © 43

festival promises an unforgettable experience. With a diverse lineup spanning various genres, from rock to electro, the Festival des Vieilles Charrues showcases both established and emerging talents. Dance to the rhythm of the music, revel in the electric atmosphere and create lifelong memories.

Festival de la Saint-Loup

In Guingamp, the Festival de la Saint-Loup takes place in August and offers a window into the region's rich Breton heritage. Celebrating Breton culture through music, dance, and traditional games, this festival brings together locals and visitors alike in a joyful atmosphere. Enjoy the melodic tunes of Breton bagpipes, witness mesmerizing traditional dances, and participate in captivating competitions such as Breton wrestling and stone lifting. The Festival de la Saint-Loup is a wonderful opportunity to

Copyrighted Material © 44

connect with the vibrant traditions and warm-hearted locals of Guingamp.

Les Transmusicales de Rennes

Rennes, the vibrant capital of Brittany, hosts one of Europe's most renowned music festivals, Les Transmusicales. Held annually in December, this event showcases emerging talents from a wide range of music genres, including rock, pop, electronic, and world music. Be prepared to discover new sounds and experience cutting-edge performances in the heart of Rennes. With its electrifying energy and eclectic lineup, Les Transmusicales promises an unforgettable musical journey.

Festival de la Danse de Saint-Malo

For dance enthusiasts, the Festival de la Danse de Saint-Malo is a must-attend event. Taking place in Saint-Malo in May, this festival gathers renowned dance companies from around the world, presenting a diverse range of styles and performances. From classical ballet to contemporary dance, immerse yourself in the beauty and grace of this captivating art form. The festival also offers workshops and masterclasses, allowing participants to engage with professional dancers and expand their skills.

Festival Photo La Gacilly

For lovers of photography and nature, the Festival Photo La Gacilly is a unique experience not to be missed. Held from June to September in the charming village of La Gacilly, this festival showcases large-scale outdoor exhibitions featuring stunning images by renowned photographers. Explore the picturesque streets adorned with captivating photographs, each telling a compelling story. With a focus on environmental themes, this festival combines art and

Copyrighted Material © 46

awareness, inspiring visitors to reflect on our relationship with the natural world.

Les Filets Bleus in Douarnenez

Similar to its namesake festival in Concarneau, Les Filets Bleus in Douarnenez pays tribute to the maritime heritage of the town. Held in August, this event features maritime-themed parades, traditional music, and captivating boat races. Dive into the lively atmosphere, browse through the bustling markets, and sample delectable seafood dishes that showcase the region's culinary excellence. Les Filets Bleus in Douarnenez is a celebration of Douarnenez's close ties to the sea and a wonderful opportunity to connect with the local maritime culture.

Brittany's festivals and events offer a gateway to the region's cultural extravaganza, providing travelers with an immersive and authentic experience. From the rhythmic beats of Celtic music at the Festival Interceltique de Lorient to the medieval charm of the Fête des Remparts de Dinan, each festival has its unique ambiance and allure. Whether you are drawn to traditional folklore, contemporary music, dance performances, or visual arts, Brittany has something to captivate every traveler's heart.

Copyrighted Material ©

111. Planning Your Trip

In this chapter, we will delve into the essentials of planning your trip to Brittany, providing you with the insights and information needed to make the most of your visit.

A. Best Time to Visit

When planning a trip to Brittany, it's essential to consider the best time to visit this beautiful region of France. Brittany offers a unique blend of stunning coastlines, charming towns, rich history, and vibrant culture. To make the most of your visit, it's important to choose a time that aligns with your interests and preferences. In this section, we will explore the different seasons in Brittany and help you determine the best time to embark on your journey.

Spring (March to May)

Spring is a fantastic time to visit Brittany, as the region blossoms with vibrant colors and mild temperatures. The landscapes come alive with blooming flowers, and the coastal areas offer breathtaking views. During this season, the tourist crowds are relatively smaller compared to the peak summer months, allowing you to enjoy a more peaceful and authentic experience. In spring, you can explore the charming towns, visit the ancient castles, and embark on scenic coastal walks without the hustle and bustle of peak tourist season.

Summer (June to August)

Summer is undoubtedly the most popular time to visit Brittany, thanks to its warm weather and long days. The region

Copyrighted Material © 50

experiences a surge in tourism during this season, and popular coastal towns like Saint-Malo and Quiberon can get quite crowded. However, the lively atmosphere, outdoor festivals, and vibrant beach scenes make up for it. If you enjoy bustling markets, water sports, and vibrant nightlife, summer might be the ideal time for your visit. Be sure to book accommodations and attractions well in advance to secure your spot during this peak season.

Autumn (September to November)

Autumn in Brittany is a breathtaking season characterized by stunning foliage, fewer crowds, and mild temperatures. The region takes on a golden hue as the leaves change colors, creating a picturesque setting for nature enthusiasts and photographers. Autumn is an ideal time to explore the countryside, go hiking along the coast, or visit charming villages without the summer crowds. Additionally, this season offers

Copyrighted Material © 51

opportunities to participate in harvest festivals and indulge in local culinary delights, including freshly harvested seafood and cider.

Winter (December to February)

While Brittany experiences colder temperatures in winter, it still holds its charm during this season. The coastal towns take on a peaceful and serene atmosphere, and you can enjoy the region's beauty without the tourist crowds. Winter is an excellent time to explore historic sites, delve into the region's rich cultural heritage, and savor hearty traditional dishes. Additionally, if you're a fan of winter sports, you'll find opportunities for activities like skiing and ice skating in certain parts of Brittany.

B. Duration of Stay

Determining the duration of your stay in Brittany depends on various factors, including your interests, available time, and the number of attractions you wish to explore. Here are some recommendations to help you plan your trip effectively:

Short Getaway (2-4 days)

If you have limited time but still want to experience the essence of Brittany, a short getaway of 2-4 days can be a great option. Focus on exploring one or two key areas such as Saint-Malo and its historic walls, the picturesque town of Dinan, or the stunning Pink Granite Coast in Perros-Guirec. This shorter duration allows you to immerse yourself in the local culture, savor the regional cuisine, and enjoy the scenic beauty of Brittany's coastlines.

Weeklong Adventure (5-7 days)

For a more in-depth exploration of Brittany, plan a weeklong adventure to fully appreciate the region's diverse offerings. You can dedicate a couple of days to visiting Rennes, the capital city, and indulge in its vibrant cultural scene. Spend a few days exploring the rugged beauty of Finistère, including the charming town of Brest and the breathtaking Crozon Peninsula. Don't miss the opportunity to visit the enchanting island of Belle-Île-en-Mer, known for its stunning cliffs and picturesque villages. A week allows you to immerse yourself in the local atmosphere, discover hidden gems, and enjoy leisurely moments along the coast.

Extended Exploration (10+ days)

If you have ample time to spare and want to delve deep into the wonders of Brittany, consider an extended exploration of 10 days or more. This duration allows you to venture beyond the popular tourist spots and

Copyrighted Material © 54

uncover the region's hidden treasures. Explore the medieval city of Vannes, wander through the mystical Forest of Brocéliande, and discover the artistic charm of Pont-Aven, known for its association with renowned painters. You can also embark on a road trip along the coast, stopping at quaint fishing villages, lighthouses, and rugged cliffs along the way. This extended stay ensures you have the opportunity to immerse yourself fully in the cultural, historical, and natural wonders of Brittany.

Remember, these recommendations are just a starting point, and you can always tailor your trip based on your interests and preferences. It's important to strike a balance between exploring popular attractions and allowing yourself time to relax and soak in the ambiance of Brittany. Whether you're a history enthusiast, a nature lover, or a foodie seeking culinary delights, Brittany offers something for everyone.

The best time to visit Brittany depends on your preferences, but each season has its unique charm. Spring and autumn offer mild temperatures, vibrant landscapes, and fewer crowds, while summer provides a lively atmosphere and beach activities. Winter presents a quieter ambiance and the opportunity to indulge in the region's cultural heritage. When it comes to the duration of your stay, it varies based on the depth of exploration you seek. Whether you have a few days or several weeks, Brittany promises a memorable experience filled with captivating landscapes, rich history, and warm hospitality.

C. Visa & Entry Requirements

If you're planning a trip to this captivating destination, it's essential to familiarize yourself with the visa and entry requirements. This comprehensive guide will provide you with accurate and concise information, ensuring a smooth and hassle-free travel experience. Read on to discover the necessary steps to enter Brittany legally and make the most of your journey.

Schengen Area & Visa Waiver Program

Schengen Area

Brittany is part of the Schengen Area, an agreement between 26 European countries that have abolished internal borders, allowing for the free movement of people within the region. As a traveler, you will need to obtain a Schengen visa, granting you access to all member countries, including France, where Brittany is located.

Visa Waiver Program

Copyrighted Material © 57

Certain nationalities are exempt from obtaining a Schengen visa due to the Visa Waiver Program. Travelers from these countries can visit Brittany and the Schengen Area for up to 90 days within 180 days without a visa. However, it's crucial to check if you meet the specific requirements and conditions of the program.

Who Needs a Schengen Visa?

Non-Visa Exempt Countries

If your country is not listed under the Visa Waiver Program, you will need to apply for a Schengen visa at the French embassy or consulate in your home country. Make sure to initiate the visa application process well in advance to allow for sufficient processing time.

Visa Category & Duration

The Schengen visa is available in various categories, including tourist, business, and transit visas. The duration of the visa can range from short-stay (up to 90 days) to long-stay (more than 90 days). For visits to Brittany for tourist or business purposes, a short-stay Schengen visa is typically sufficient.

Applying for a Schengen Visa

Required Documents

The following documents must be presented to apply for a Schengen visa:

1. Completed visa application form

2. The passport must be valid for at least three months beyond the desired stay.

3. Recent passport-sized photographs

4. Travel itinerary, including accommodation and return flight details

5. evidence of travel insurance with at least €30,000 in coverage

6. Proof of financial means to cover your stay in Brittany

7. Invitation letter (if applicable)

8. Supporting documents based on the purpose of your visit (e.g., business or tourism)

Visa Application Process

Contact the French embassy or consulate in your country to obtain the precise visa application requirements and procedures. Complete the application form completely, and then send it together with the necessary paperwork. Pay the visa fee, which varies

Copyrighted Material ©

according to your country of citizenship. If required, make time to meet for a visa interview. You will be informed of the visa decision following the processing of your application.

Traveling with Children

If you plan to travel to Brittany with children, additional documents may be required. Minors must have their passports and, if applicable, birth certificates. If traveling with only one parent or without parents, a consent letter signed by the absent parent(s) or legal guardian(s) is necessary. It's advisable to check the specific requirements to avoid any complications during your journey.

Border Control & Entry Regulations

Passport Validity

Make sure your passport is still valid for at least three months after the day you intend to leave the Schengen Zone. It's crucial to check your passport's expiration date and renew it if necessary before your trip to Brittany.

Border Control & Entry Process

Upon arrival in Brittany or any other Schengen country, you will go through border control. Have your passport and other travel documents ready for inspection by the immigration officers. They may ask you questions about the purpose of your visit, the duration of your stay, and your accommodation details. Be honest and provide accurate information to ensure a smooth entry process.

Entry Requirements

To enter Brittany or any other Schengen country, you must meet the following requirements:

1. Possess a valid passport that meets the minimum validity criteria.

2. Have a valid Schengen visa, if applicable.

3. Show evidence that you have the resources necessary to pay for your stay.

4. Show evidence of return or onward travel (such as a return flight ticket).

5. Have travel insurance with adequate coverage for medical emergencies.

6. Comply with the regulations and restrictions imposed by the Schengen Area and French authorities.

Copyrighted Material © 63

Extending Your Stay

If you wish to extend your stay in Brittany beyond the allowed duration of your Schengen visa, you must contact the local French immigration authorities before your visa expires. Extensions are granted only in exceptional circumstances, such as unforeseen medical emergencies or force majeure events. It's crucial to adhere to the visa regulations to avoid any legal complications.

COVID-19 Travel Requirements

In response to the global COVID-19 pandemic, travel restrictions and health protocols may be in place. Before traveling to Brittany, stay informed about the latest travel advisories, entry requirements, and health guidelines issued by the French government and health authorities. These may include providing proof of vaccination, negative COVID-19 test results, or

Copyrighted Material © 64

undergoing quarantine upon arrival. Regularly check official sources for updates and comply with the requirements for a safe and responsible journey.

As you plan your trip to Brittany, understanding the visa and entry requirements is crucial to ensure a seamless travel experience. By familiarizing yourself with the Schengen visa process, necessary documents, and entry regulations, you can avoid any last-minute complications. Remember to stay updated on any travel advisories and COVID-19 protocols to prioritize your safety. Now, pack your bags, immerse yourself in the beauty of Brittany, and create unforgettable memories in this enchanting region of France.

D. Health & Safety

This comprehensive guide also aims to equip you with the knowledge and precautions necessary to ensure a smooth and enjoyable journey. From pre-trip preparations to on-the-road safety measures, we'll cover every aspect, offering expert advice and practical tips to enhance your travel experience. Let's dive in!

Pre-Trip Preparations

Research Your Destination

1. Familiarize yourself with the local customs, laws, and medical facilities.

2. Check travel advisories and register with your embassy if necessary.

3. Understand the prevalent health risks and vaccination requirements.

Consult Your Healthcare Provider

1. Schedule a visit to assess your overall health and discuss any specific concerns.

2. Review your vaccination status and receive the necessary immunizations.

3. Discuss any required medications or prescriptions, including potential interactions.

Get Travel Insurance

1. Invest in comprehensive travel insurance that covers medical emergencies, trip cancellations, and lost belongings.

2. Understand the policy's terms and conditions and keep a copy of the insurance details accessible during your trip.

Prepare a First-Aid Kit

Copyrighted Material © 67

1. Pack essential medical supplies such as bandages, antiseptics, pain relievers, and any prescribed medications.

2. Include personal items like insect repellent, sunscreen, and any necessary allergy medication.

Safe Travel Practices

Practice Good Hygiene

1. Wash your hands frequently with soap and water, especially before meals and after using public facilities.

2. Carry hand sanitizer with at least 60% alcohol content for times when hand washing isn't available.

Stay Hydrated & Eat Well

Copyrighted Material © 68

1. Drink plenty of water to stay hydrated, especially in hot climates or during physical activities.

2. Consume balanced meals to maintain your energy levels and support your immune system.

3. Be cautious when consuming street food, ensuring it is freshly prepared and from reputable vendors.

Protect Yourself from Sunburn

1. Wear sunscreen with a high SPF and reapply regularly, especially if swimming or sweating.

2. Use protective clothing, hats, and sunglasses to shield yourself from harmful UV rays.

3. When the sun is at its strongest (often between 10 am and 4 pm), seek cover.

Copyrighted Material © 69

Be Cautious with Water & Food

1. Only consume water from trusted sources. If unsure, use bottled water or boil tap water before drinking.

2. Avoid consuming raw or undercooked food, unpasteurized dairy products, and unpeeled fruits or vegetables.

3. Use caution with ice cubes, as they may be made from contaminated water.

Practice Safe Transportation

1. Choose reputable transportation providers with good safety records.

2. Wear seatbelts in cars and helmets on bikes or motorbikes.

Copyrighted Material ©

3. Be vigilant and aware of your surroundings while using public transportation.

Protect Against Insect-Borne Illnesses

1. Use insect repellent containing DEET, picaridin, or other recommended ingredients.

2. Wear long sleeves, pants, and socks in areas prone to mosquitoes or other biting insects.

3. Consider bed nets or screens to protect against mosquito bites while sleeping.

Emergency Preparedness

Know Emergency Contact Information

1. Carry a list of emergency phone numbers, including local authorities,

Copyrighted Material © 71

your embassy, and your insurance provider.

2. Save important contact information on your phone or in a portable document format (PDF).

Share Your Itinerary

1. Inform a trusted friend or family member about your travel plans, including destinations, and accommodations.

2. Provide them with copies of your travel documents, such as your passport and travel insurance details.

Stay Informed

1. Keep track of local news and weather updates to be aware of any potential risks or emergencies.

Copyrighted Material © 72

2. Monitor travel advisories and register with your embassy or consulate for important alerts or assistance.

Familiarize Yourself with Basic First Aid

1. Enroll in a basic first aid course or educate yourself on essential first aid procedures.

2. Learn how to administer CPR, treat minor injuries, and recognize signs of more serious medical conditions.

Carry a Travel Medical Kit

1. Include items such as adhesive bandages, antiseptic wipes, pain relievers, antidiarrheal medication, and any necessary prescription medications.

Copyrighted Material © 73

2. Add emergency supplies like a flashlight, whistle, and waterproof matches.

Cultural Sensitivity & Respect

Respect Local Customs & Traditions

1. Research and understand the cultural norms, values, and traditions of your destination.

2. Dress modestly and appropriately, particularly when visiting religious or conservative areas.

3. Behave respectfully in sacred or culturally significant sites.

Be Mindful of Photography

1. Seek permission before taking photos of individuals, particularly in sensitive or private settings.

Copyrighted Material © 74

2. Respect photography restrictions in museums, religious sites, and other designated areas.

Learn Basic Local Phrases

1. Make an effort to learn a few key phrases in the local language, such as greetings, thank you, and please.

2. Locals appreciate the effort, and it helps foster positive interactions and cultural exchange.

Practice Responsible Tourism

1. Minimize your environmental impact by avoiding littering, supporting eco-friendly practices, and respecting wildlife and natural habitats.

Copyrighted Material © 75

2. Engage in ethical activities and tours that promote sustainable tourism and benefit local communities.

COVID-19 Considerations

Stay Informed & Follow Guidelines

1. Stay updated on the latest COVID-19 guidelines and travel restrictions issued by local authorities and international health organizations.

2. Adhere to mask-wearing, physical distancing, and hygiene protocols, both during travel and at your destination.

Get Vaccinated

1. Follow the recommended vaccination guidelines for COVID-19 in your home country.

Copyrighted Material © 76

2. Research the vaccination requirements and recommendations for your travel destination.

Carry Necessary Safety Supplies

1. Pack extra face masks, hand sanitizer, and disinfectant wipes to ensure you have sufficient supplies during your journey.

2. Consider portable UV sterilizers or disinfectant sprays for added protection.

Be Flexible & Prepared for Changes

1. Be aware that travel restrictions and guidelines may change at short notice.

2. Have backup plans and be prepared to adjust your itinerary or return home if necessary.

Copyrighted Material © 77

By prioritizing your health and safety, you can make the most of your travel experiences while minimizing potential risks. Remember to plan, stay informed, and follow local guidelines and customs. By practicing good hygiene, being mindful of your surroundings, and taking necessary precautions, you can have a safe and enjoyable journey. Embrace the diversity of cultures, engage in responsible tourism, and create lasting memories. Bon voyage!

E. Currency & Money Matters

This part aims to provide you with accurate and concise information, ensuring a smooth financial experience during your stay. From currency exchange options to payment methods, we'll cover everything you need to know to navigate the monetary landscape in Brittany.

Currency in Brittany

In Brittany, the official currency is the Euro (€), which is the same as the rest of France and many other European countries. As the Euro is widely accepted throughout the region, you won't encounter any difficulties using it for your transactions.

Currency Exchange

To obtain Euros for your trip, you have several options for currency exchange in Brittany. Here are the most common methods:

★ Banks: Banks in Brittany offer currency exchange services, and you'll find branches in most towns and cities. They generally provide competitive exchange rates, but it's advisable to check their fees and commissions beforehand. Some banks may require you to have an account with them to exchange money.

★ Exchange Offices: Currency exchange offices, known as bureaux de change, are also available in major tourist areas and transportation hubs. While their rates may vary, it's wise to compare offers from different exchange offices to secure the best rate. Be aware that some exchange offices may charge higher fees or commissions.

★ ATMs: Automated Teller Machines (ATMs) are widely available throughout Brittany. They offer a convenient way to withdraw cash in Euros using your debit or credit card. However, it's crucial to check with your bank about any foreign transaction fees or withdrawal limits that may apply. Remember to use ATMs located in secure areas and be cautious of skimming devices.

Copyrighted Material © 80

Payment Methods

When it comes to making payments in Brittany, you'll find a range of accepted payment methods. Here are the most common ones:

★ Cash: Carrying some cash is always advisable for small purchases, market visits, or places that might not accept cards. Many businesses, particularly smaller establishments, prefer cash transactions. Ensure you have a mix of smaller denominations for convenience.

★ Credit and Debit Cards: Credit and debit cards are widely accepted in hotels, restaurants, shops, and larger establishments in Brittany. The most widely used credit cards are Visa and Mastercard, followed by American Express and Diners Club. However, it's always good to have some cash on

Copyrighted Material © 81

hand, as some establishments may not accept cards for smaller transactions or in remote areas.

★ Contactless Payments: Contactless payment methods, such as Apple Pay, Google Pay, or Samsung Pay, are increasingly popular in Brittany. Many merchants, including cafes, restaurants, and supermarkets, have adopted this convenient and secure payment option. Look for the contactless symbol on card readers to check if it's available.

★ Traveler's Checks: While traveler's checks used to be a popular option in the past, their acceptance has significantly diminished in recent years. Many establishments no longer accept them, and it can be challenging to find places to cash them. It's advisable to consider alternative

Copyrighted Material © 82

payment methods for your convenience.

★ Mobile Payment Apps: Mobile payment apps like PayPal or local French options such as Lydia or Paylib are becoming more prevalent in Brittany. They allow you to link your bank account or credit card to make easy and secure transactions using your smartphone. Make sure to check if the app is compatible with your device and if it's accepted in the places you plan to visit.

Tipping Etiquette

Tipping in Brittany is not obligatory, as service charges are generally included in the bill. However, it's customary to leave a small tip as a token of appreciation for good service. Following are some suggestions for tipping:

Copyrighted Material © 83

★ Restaurants: If you're satisfied with the service, leaving a 5-10% tip is a common practice. You can either leave the cash on the table or tell the waiter the amount you wish to add to the bill when paying by card.

★ Cafés and Bars: It's not customary to tip at cafés or bars, but you can round up the bill or leave some small change as a gesture of appreciation.

★ Taxi Drivers: It's customary to round up the fare to the nearest Euro or add a small tip if the driver has been helpful or provided exceptional service.

★ Hotel Staff: While not obligatory, you may choose to tip hotel staff, such as porters or housekeeping, for their assistance. A small amount, typically 1-2 Euros per service, is appreciated.

Copyrighted Material © 84

Safety & Security

When it comes to handling money and ensuring your financial security in Brittany, it's essential to keep the following tips in mind:

★ Be vigilant at ATMs: When using ATMs, be cautious of your surroundings and ensure the machine is in a well-lit, secure area. Look out for any suspicious devices attached to the ATM that may compromise your card or personal information.

★ Keep an eye on your belongings: Petty theft can occur in crowded places, so keep your wallet, purse, and other valuables secure. Avoid displaying large sums of cash in public and consider using a money belt or a secure travel wallet to keep your money and cards safe.

Copyrighted Material ©

★ Inform your bank: Before traveling to Brittany, notify your bank or credit card company about your trip. This will help prevent any unexpected issues with card transactions or withdrawals.

★ Use secure Wi-Fi networks: When making online payments or accessing your banking apps, ensure you're connected to a secure Wi-Fi network, preferably one provided by your hotel or a reputable establishment. Public Wi-Fi networks may pose security risks, so exercise caution.

★ Keep emergency contact information: Note down the contact numbers for your bank, credit card companies, and embassy or consulate. In case of any issues or loss of cards, you can quickly reach out for assistance.

★ Purchase travel insurance: Consider obtaining comprehensive travel insurance that covers medical emergencies, loss or theft of personal belongings, and trip cancellations. This will provide financial protection and peace of mind during your journey.

Understanding the currency and money matters in Brittany is crucial for a hassle-free and secure trip. By familiarizing yourself with the local currency, exchange options, payment methods, tipping etiquette, and safety precautions, you'll be well-prepared to manage your finances during your stay. Remember to prioritize your security by taking necessary precautions and staying alert. Enjoy your time exploring the beautiful region of Brittany and have a wonderful trip!

Copyrighted Material ©

IV. Exploring The Regions

Brittany, also known as Bretagne, is a beautiful region located in the northwest of France. It is known for its stunning coastline, rich history, Celtic heritage, and unique cultural traditions. If you're planning to explore Brittany, here are some regions and places you should consider visiting

A. Finistère

Welcome to the captivating region of Finistère in Brittany, France! Nestled on the westernmost point of the country, Finistère boasts stunning coastlines, charming towns, and a rich cultural heritage that is sure to leave you mesmerized. In this comprehensive guide, we will take you on a virtual journey through three remarkable destinations in Finistère: Brest, Quimper, and Concarneau. Prepare to immerse yourself in the unique charm, natural beauty, and historical significance of each location. Whether you're a history enthusiast, a nature lover, or a food connoisseur, Finistère has something for everyone. Let's begin our exploration!

Brest: A Maritime Hub

Brest, a vibrant coastal city, is renowned for its maritime heritage, lively atmosphere, and breathtaking scenery. As you arrive in Brest, be sure to visit the iconic Brest Castle. This 11th-century fortress offers panoramic views of the city and the enchanting harbor. Take a stroll along the Quai de la Douane, lined with quaint cafes and boutiques, where you can savor local delicacies and shop for unique souvenirs.

For maritime enthusiasts, the National Maritime Museum is a must-visit. It houses

Copyrighted Material © 89

an impressive collection of artifacts, model ships, and interactive exhibits that trace the region's maritime history. Don't miss the opportunity to explore the imposing naval vessels at the nearby Port de Plaisance, which offers an up-close look at modern maritime technology.

Nature lovers will find solace in the stunning coastline surrounding Brest. The Plage du Moulin Blanc is a picturesque beach where you can unwind, bask in the sun, or indulge in water sports. For a more adventurous experience, head to the Parc Naturel Régional d'Armorique, a vast nature reserve offering hiking trails, wildlife observation, and breathtaking vistas.

Quimper: A Timeless Beauty

Quimper, the cultural capital of Finistère, exudes an old-world charm that transports you back in time. Known for its well-preserved medieval architecture and

Copyrighted Material © 90

traditional crafts, Quimper is a treasure trove of history and culture. Begin your exploration at the heart of the city, in the enchanting Old Town.

Wander through the cobbled streets and admire the half-timbered houses adorned with colorful flowers. The Gothic-style Quimper Cathedral, with its magnificent stained glass windows, is a true masterpiece. Take a moment to visit the Musée des Beaux-Arts, home to a splendid collection of paintings and sculptures from various periods.

No visit to Quimper is complete without exploring its renowned pottery. The Faïence de Quimper is famous worldwide for its distinctive hand-painted designs. Visit the HB-Henriot workshop to witness the skillful craftsmanship and learn about the intricate process behind these iconic pieces. You can even try your hand at painting your ceramic masterpiece!

Copyrighted Material © 91

Venture outside the city to discover the idyllic countryside of Quimper. The Odet River, known as the most beautiful river in France, offers tranquil boat rides amidst lush greenery and charming villages. A visit to the Jardin de la Retraite, a peaceful public garden, allows you to unwind in nature's embrace and admire the vibrant floral displays.

Concarneau: A Seaside Gem

Concarneau, a picturesque coastal town, is renowned for its fortified old town and bustling fishing port. As you step foot in Concarneau, you'll be greeted by the mighty walls of the Ville Close, a fortified island that transports you back to medieval times. Take a stroll along its ramparts and immerse yourself in the history that permeates its narrow streets. The Musée de la Ville Close, located within the walls, offers a fascinating

Copyrighted Material © 92

glimpse into the town's past through its exhibits and artifacts.

For seafood enthusiasts, a visit to the bustling fishing port is a must. Watch as local fishermen unload their catch of the day, and sample fresh, succulent seafood at one of the charming waterfront restaurants. Don't forget to try the famous Concarneau sardines, a local specialty that tantalizes the taste buds with its rich flavor.

Concarneau also offers beautiful sandy beaches where you can relax, soak up the sun, and take refreshing dips in the azure waters of the Atlantic Ocean. Plage des Sables Blancs and Plage de Cornouaille are two popular spots that offer a perfect blend of relaxation and natural beauty.

If you're interested in maritime history, visit the Fishing Museum to learn about the town's long-standing fishing traditions and the importance of the sea to Concarneau's identity. The museum showcases an extensive collection of fishing gear, boats, and historical artifacts that provide insight into the region's maritime heritage.

Culinary Delights & Local Cuisine

Finistère is a gastronomic paradise, offering a diverse array of flavors and culinary delights. Indulge your taste buds with the region's renowned seafood dishes, including the freshest oysters, succulent lobster, and mouthwatering scallops. Pair your seafood feast with a glass of crisp local cider or a chilled Muscadet wine to complement the flavors perfectly.

Don't miss the opportunity to try the iconic Breton crêpes and galettes. These delicious pancakes, made from buckwheat flour, can be enjoyed with a variety of savory or sweet fillings, such as cheese, ham, caramelized apples, or homemade salted caramel. Be sure to visit a traditional crêperie in each

Copyrighted Material © 94

destination to savor their unique interpretations of this beloved dish.

For cheese lovers, Finistère offers an impressive selection of regional cheeses. From the pungent and creamy Pont-l'Évêque to the tangy and flavorful Gouda-like Mimolette, there is a cheese to suit every palate. Visit local markets, such as the Halles Saint Louis in Brest or the Halles de Cornouaille in Quimper, to discover a wide range of artisanal cheeses and other local delicacies.

Festivals & Cultural Events

Finistère is known for its vibrant festivals and cultural events that celebrate the region's heritage and traditions. Throughout the year, you can witness colorful parades, live music performances, and traditional dances that showcase the local culture.

Copyrighted Material © 95

In Brest, the Festival des Vieilles Charrues is a highlight for music lovers, attracting renowned artists from various genres. Quimper hosts the Festival de Cornouaille, a celebration of Breton culture featuring traditional music, dance, and folkloric performances. Concarneau's a Fête des Filets Bleus, held annually, is a lively event where you can experience Breton customs, enjoy street entertainment, and taste local delicacies.

Sustainable Tourism

As you explore Finistère's natural beauty, remember to be a responsible traveler. Follow designated trails, avoid littering, and support local businesses that promote sustainability and eco-friendly practices.

Finistère, with its captivating coastal landscapes, historical treasures, and culinary delights, is a region that offers a truly immersive and unforgettable

Copyrighted Material © 96

experience. From the maritime hub of Brest to the timeless beauty of Quimper and the seaside charm of Concarneau, each destination has its unique allure.

B. Côtes-d'Armor

Welcome to the captivating region of Côtes-d'Armor, located in the beautiful Brittany region of France. Here, you will find a perfect blend of breathtaking landscapes, rich history, and charming towns. In this comprehensive guide, we will take you on a journey through three must-visit destinations in Côtes-d'Armor: Saint-Brieuc, Dinan, and Perros-Guirec. Each of these towns has its unique character and attractions, promising an unforgettable experience for every traveler. So, without further ado, let's dive into the wonders of Côtes-d'Armor!

Saint-Brieuc

Copyrighted Material © 97

Located on the northern coast of Côtes-d'Armor, Saint-Brieuc is the capital city of the department and offers a delightful mix of history, culture, and natural beauty.

Historical Charm

Saint-Brieuc boasts a rich history dating back to medieval times, evident in its architecture and historical landmarks. The Gothic-style Saint-Étienne Cathedral stands proudly in the city center, showcasing intricate sculptures and stunning stained glass windows. Explore the medieval streets, lined with half-timbered houses, and discover hidden gems like the historic Place du Chai and the beautiful Fosse-aux-Lions garden.

Cultural Treasures

Immerse yourself in the local culture by visiting the Musée d'Art et d'Histoire de

Saint-Brieuc, which houses an impressive collection of artwork and artifacts. Don't miss the opportunity to experience the vibrant atmosphere of the weekly Saint-Brieuc Market, where you can sample regional delicacies and buy unique souvenirs. For a touch of entertainment, catch a performance at the Grand Théâtre, which hosts a variety of cultural events throughout the year.

Natural Splendor

Nature lovers will be enchanted by the breathtaking landscapes surrounding Saint-Brieuc. Take a stroll along the stunning Plérin beach, known for its golden sands and panoramic views of the coastline. Explore the picturesque Bay of Saint-Brieuc, a paradise for birdwatchers, where you can spot numerous species of migratory birds. For a more adventurous experience, head to the nearby Les Chaos du Gouët, a scenic hiking trail that leads you through

Copyrighted Material © 99

impressive rock formations and dense forests.

Dinan

Nestled along the banks of the Rance River, Dinan is a charming medieval town that exudes a romantic atmosphere. With its well-preserved architecture and enchanting streets, Dinan offers a glimpse into the past.

Medieval Marvels

Step back in time as you wander through Dinan's medieval heart. The centerpiece is the magnificent Château de Dinan, an imposing fortress that offers panoramic views of the town and the river. Explore the cobbled streets of the old town, lined with half-timbered houses, artisan shops, and quaint cafes. Don't miss the opportunity to walk along the famous Rue du Jerzual, a steep street adorned with colorful flowers and charming boutiques.

Copyrighted Material © 100

Rich Heritage

Dinan is home to a wealth of historical treasures. Discover the Basilique Saint-Sauveur, a beautiful church showcasing a mix of Romanesque and Gothic styles. Visit the Musée du Château de Dinan, located within the castle, to learn about the town's fascinating history through its extensive collection of artifacts. Be sure to explore the ramparts, which offer a scenic walkway with panoramic views of the river and the surrounding countryside.

River Adventures

Experience the tranquil beauty of the Rance River by embarking on a boat trip or kayak excursion. Cruise along the river, passing picturesque landscapes and charming villages. Admire the impressive 19th-century viaduct, Pont de Dinan, which spans the river and adds to the town's charm. If you're

Copyrighted Material © 101

feeling adventurous, rent a bike and follow the scenic Rance River Trail, which will lead you through lush greenery and offer breathtaking views at every turn.

Perros-Guirec

Perros-Guirec, located on the Pink Granite Coast, is a coastal gem that will leave you spellbound with its unique rock formations, sandy beaches, and rugged beauty.

Pink Granite Coast

The Pink Granite Coast is one of the most remarkable natural wonders in Côtes-d'Armor, and Perros-Guirec is the perfect base to explore its beauty. Take a stroll along the Sentier des Douaniers (Customs Officer's Path), a scenic coastal trail that winds its way through the stunning pink granite rocks and offers breathtaking views of the emerald sea. Marvel at the famous Ploumanac'h lighthouse, perched

Copyrighted Material © 102

atop the granite cliffs, and capture the magical sunset over the rugged coastline.

Beaches & Water Sports

Perros-Guirec boasts a selection of pristine sandy beaches, inviting you to relax and soak up the sun. Trestraou Beach is a popular choice, offering calm waters and a vibrant promenade lined with restaurants and cafes. For adventure seekers, indulge in a range of water sports, including kayaking, paddleboarding, and sailing. The crystal-clear waters provide the perfect backdrop for snorkeling and diving enthusiasts to explore marine life.

Île de Bréhat

Embark on a short boat ride from Perros-Guirec to Île de Bréhat, a stunning archipelago renowned for its natural beauty. Explore the car-free island by foot or bicycle, discovering its charming villages,

Copyrighted Material ©

colorful gardens, and scenic coastal paths. Admire the blooming flowers and exotic plants at the Jardin Georges Delaselle, a botanical garden showcasing a vast collection of species from around the world. With its tranquil ambiance and unspoiled landscapes, Île de Bréhat is a true paradise for nature lovers.

Côtes-d'Armor offers a diverse range of experiences for every traveler, and the towns of Saint-Brieuc, Dinan, and Perros-Guirec exemplify the region's allure. From the historical charm of Saint-Brieuc to the medieval splendor of Dinan and the natural beauty of Perros-Guirec, each destination presents its unique treasures to explore. Whether you are captivated by history, culture, outdoor adventures, or simply the breathtaking landscapes, Côtes-d'Armor will leave you with unforgettable memories.

Copyrighted Material © 104

C. Ille-et-Vilaine

Welcome to Ille-et-Vilaine, a captivating department nestled in the Brittany region of France. Known for its rich history, picturesque landscapes, and vibrant culture, Ille-et-Vilaine is a treasure trove waiting to be discovered. In this part, we will take you on an unforgettable journey through its three iconic destinations: Rennes, Saint-Malo, and Fougères. Each city offers a unique blend of attractions, historical landmarks, and authentic experiences, making Ille-et-Vilaine a must-visit destination for travelers seeking a taste of both the past and the present.

Rennes

Situated in the heart of Ille-et-Vilaine, Rennes is the capital city and a vibrant hub of art, history, and gastronomy. Steeped in medieval charm, Rennes effortlessly

Copyrighted Material © 105

combines its ancient heritage with a modern, cosmopolitan atmosphere.

Old Town (Rennes Ville Historique)

Start your exploration in the enchanting Old Town, where narrow cobblestone streets wind their way through half-timbered houses and stunning architectural marvels. The Place des Lices, a bustling square renowned for its weekly market, offers a glimpse into the city's vibrant local life.

Parliament of Brittany (Parlement de Bretagne)

Marvel at the magnificent Parliament of Brittany, a symbol of Rennes' rich history. This striking 17th-century building boasts exquisite architectural details and houses the Court of Appeals.

Thabor Park (Parc du Thabor)

Copyrighted Material © 106

Escape the city's hustle and bustle and find tranquility in the beautiful Thabor Park. This expansive green oasis features meticulously manicured gardens, serene ponds, and charming pathways. Don't miss the stunning rose garden, which bursts with vibrant colors during the summer months.

Saint-Malo

Nestled along the Emerald Coast, Saint-Malo exudes a captivating maritime spirit. With its fortified walls, stunning beaches, and lively atmosphere, this coastal gem invites you to immerse yourself in its rich seafaring history.

Intra-Muros

Step into the walled city of Intra-Muros and transport yourself back in time. The narrow streets lined with stone buildings house quaint boutiques, cozy cafes, and exceptional seafood restaurants. Climb to the top of the ramparts for breathtaking panoramic views of the sea.

Fort National

Take a short boat ride to the nearby Fort National, a historic fortress perched on a rocky islet. This imposing structure offers a fascinating glimpse into Saint-Malo's defensive past, with its network of tunnels and stunning coastal views.

Grand Aquarium

For a unique underwater adventure, visit the Grand Aquarium. Explore a mesmerizing array of marine life, from colorful tropical fish to majestic sharks, and learn about the importance of marine conservation through interactive exhibits.

Fougères

Nestled in the northeastern part of Ille-et-Vilaine, Fougères captivates visitors with its medieval charm and remarkable architectural heritage. Discover the city's rich history as you wander through its well-preserved medieval streets.

Fougères Castle (Château de Fougères)

Begin your journey in Fougères with a visit to its magnificent castle. This impressive fortress is one of the largest medieval strongholds in Europe and offers breathtaking views from its ramparts. Explore the maze of towers, walls, and courtyards, and delve into the castle's history through engaging exhibitions.

Public Garden (Jardin Public)

Escape to the tranquil oasis of the Public Garden, a lush green space in the heart of Fougères. Stroll along its peaceful pathways, surrounded by vibrant flowers, manicured lawns, and charming statues. Find a shaded spot to relax and immerse yourself in the serene ambiance of this idyllic retreat.

Saint-Sulpice Church

Immerse yourself in Fougères' religious heritage with a visit to the Saint-Sulpice Church. This stunning Gothic masterpiece showcases intricate architectural details and houses beautiful stained glass windows. Take a moment to admire the peaceful atmosphere and appreciate the spiritual significance of this historic place of worship.

Gastronomic Delights

No journey through Ille-et-Vilaine would be complete without indulging in its delectable culinary offerings. From fresh seafood to savory crepes, the region's gastronomy is a true delight for the senses.

Galettes & Crêpes

Copyrighted Material ©

Savor the local specialty of galettes and crêpes, a beloved Breton tradition. These mouthwatering creations can be enjoyed in cozy creperies scattered throughout Rennes, Saint-Malo, and Fougères. Whether filled with savory ingredients like cheese, ham, and eggs or sweet toppings such as Nutella or caramel, these thin pancakes are sure to satisfy your taste buds.

Seafood

Being situated along the Brittany coast, Ille-et-Vilaine is a paradise for seafood enthusiasts. Indulge in freshly caught oysters, mussels, and prawns, served with a squeeze of lemon and a glass of crisp Muscadet wine. Local seafood restaurants in Rennes, Saint-Malo, and Fougères offer a wide selection of dishes, allowing you to savor the flavors of the sea.

Cider & Galette-Saucisse

Copyrighted Material © 111

Pair your culinary adventures with a refreshing glass of Breton cider, a traditional apple-based beverage. Experience the quintessential Breton street food delight, the galette-saucisse, a warm buckwheat pancake filled with savory sausage. Join the locals in enjoying this flavorful combination, often found at food stalls and festivals throughout the region.

Ille-et-Vilaine, with its captivating cities of Rennes, Saint-Malo, and Fougères, offers a delightful blend of history, natural beauty, and culinary delights. Whether you're exploring the medieval streets of Rennes, strolling along the ramparts of Saint-Malo, or immersing yourself in the ancient charm of Fougères, each destination promises a unique and enriching experience. From architectural marvels and historic sites to tranquil gardens and mouth watering cuisine, Ille-et-Vilaine invites you to embark

Copyrighted Material © 112

on a remarkable journey through the heart of Brittany.

D. Morbihan

Welcome to the captivating region of Morbihan, nestled in the heart of Brittany, France. With its rich history, breathtaking landscapes, and unique cultural heritage, Morbihan is a dream destination for travelers seeking an authentic and immersive experience. In this guide, we will embark on a journey to discover the hidden gems of Morbihan, focusing on three remarkable places: Vannes, Carnac, and Belle-Île-en-Mer. Prepare to be enchanted as we delve into the wonders of each location, providing you with all the essential information to make your visit truly unforgettable.

Vannes: A Medieval Marvel

Our journey commences in Vannes, the capital city of Morbihan, renowned for its beautifully preserved medieval charm. Enclosed by ancient ramparts, Vannes offers a captivating blend of history, architecture, and cultural treasures. Begin your exploration at the Porte Saint-Vincent, an imposing gate that leads to the historic center. Stroll along the cobblestone streets lined with half-timbered houses, admire the elegant Gothic cathedral of Saint-Pierre, and wander through the picturesque squares brimming with cafes and boutiques. Don't miss the opportunity to visit the Château de l'Hermine, a magnificent castle that once housed the Dukes of Brittany and now hosts cultural events.

Vannes is also a city of gardens and green spaces. Take a leisurely walk along the stunning Marle Promenade, offering breathtaking views of the Gulf of Morbihan. Immerse yourself in nature at the Jardins des Remparts, a tranquil oasis nestled

Copyrighted Material © 114

within the city walls. For history enthusiasts, the Cohue Museum is a must-visit, showcasing a remarkable collection of art and artifacts from Vannes' past. In the evening, indulge in the city's vibrant culinary scene, savoring delicious seafood and traditional Breton cuisine.

Carnac: Mysteries of the Megaliths

Our next destination transports us to the enigmatic realm of Carnac, a place steeped in ancient legends and home to one of the world's most impressive megalithic sites. Brace yourself for a journey back in time as you explore the breathtaking alignments of menhirs that dot the landscape. Marvel at the sheer magnitude of these standing stones, some dating back over 6,000 years, and ponder the mysteries surrounding their construction.

Carnac is divided into three main areas: the Alignments of Kermario, the Alignments of

Kerlescan, and the Alignments of Menec. Take your time to wander through these sites, admiring the majestic stones and contemplating the cultural significance they held for our ancestors. The Museum of Prehistory provides a deeper understanding of the megalithic culture, displaying archaeological finds and offering fascinating insights into the lives of the people who built these remarkable monuments.

Beyond the megaliths, Carnac offers a charming seaside ambiance. Enjoy the sandy beaches, take a stroll along the promenade, or indulge in water sports. The town itself boasts a lively atmosphere with bustling markets, cozy cafes, and delightful restaurants. Don't forget to savor some local delicacies, such as the famous Breton crepes and cider.

Belle-Île-en-Mer: Island Paradise

Our final destination takes us to the picturesque Belle-Île-en-Mer, the largest of the Breton islands and a true haven for nature lovers. Accessible by ferry from the mainland, Belle-Île-en-Mer offers a serene escape from the hustle and bustle of everyday life. As you arrive on the island, you'll be greeted by breathtaking cliffs, pristine beaches, and idyllic landscapes that have inspired countless artists and writers.

Begin your exploration in Le Palais, the island's main town and port. Admire the charming harbor filled with colorful boats and visit the imposing Vauban Citadel, a fortress that once protected the island from invasions. Stroll through the narrow streets lined with quaint shops and art galleries, and be sure to sample the local seafood specialties at one of the cozy restaurants.

One of the highlights of Belle-Île-en-Mer is its stunning coastline. Explore the rugged beauty of Port Coton, famous for its

Copyrighted Material © 117

impressive rock formations and crashing waves that inspired the renowned painter Claude Monet. For a more tranquil experience, head to Plage de Donnant, a picturesque sandy beach perfect for sunbathing and swimming in crystal-clear waters.

Nature enthusiasts will find solace in the island's diverse landscapes. Embark on a hike along the coastal paths, where you'll be treated to breathtaking views of cliffs, hidden coves, and the vastness of the Atlantic Ocean. The Sentier des Douaniers, also known as the Customs Officer's Path, is a must-visit trail that offers panoramic vistas at every turn.

Belle-Île-en-Mer is also home to charming villages that exude a timeless charm. Visit Sauzon, a picturesque fishing village with colorful houses and a charming harbor. Take a leisurely walk along the waterfront, enjoy the local seafood, and soak in the

Copyrighted Material ©

tranquil atmosphere. Another gem is Bangor, a quaint village known for its traditional Breton architecture and peaceful ambiance. Don't miss the opportunity to explore the island's lighthouses, including the iconic Phare de Goulphar, which offers spectacular views from its clifftop location.

As you bid farewell to Belle-Île-en-Mer, take a moment to appreciate the tranquility and natural beauty that surrounds you. The island's unique blend of landscapes, vibrant culture, and warm hospitality will leave an indelible mark on your heart.

In this chapter, we have explored the captivating destinations of Morbihan, introducing you to the medieval marvel of Vannes, the mystical megaliths of Carnac, and the island paradise of Belle-Île-en-Mer. Each place offers a distinct experience, from wandering through historical streets and fortresses to pondering the mysteries of

Copyrighted Material © 119

ancient civilizations and embracing the serenity of unspoiled nature.

V. Must-See Attractions

This chapter is here to guide you on an enchanting journey through some of the region's most remarkable historical sites, natural wonders, museums, and galleries

A. Historical Sites

From the awe-inspiring Mont Saint-Michel to the mighty Saint-Malo Ramparts and the mysterious Carnac Megaliths, each destination will transport you back in time. So, fasten your seatbelts and get ready to explore Brittany's must-see historical attractions. Let the adventure begin!

Mont Saint-Michel

Copyrighted Material © 121

Our first stop on this historical voyage is the magnificent Mont Saint-Michel, an iconic UNESCO World Heritage site. Rising majestically from the sea, this medieval abbey and village are a testament to human ingenuity and architectural brilliance.

Mont Saint-Michel is located on a rocky island near the border between Brittany and Normandy. As you approach the island, its silhouette stands proudly against the horizon, creating an atmosphere of anticipation and wonder. Once inside, immerse yourself in the narrow winding streets, lined with charming shops and restaurants that evoke the ambiance of a bygone era.

At the heart of Mont Saint-Michel lies the Abbey of Mont Saint-Michel, a marvel of Gothic architecture. Take a guided tour to uncover the abbey's fascinating history, from its humble beginnings as a simple chapel to its transformation into a powerful

Benedictine abbey. Marvel at the soaring spires, intricate stained glass windows, and labyrinthine cloisters as you step back in time.

As you ascend to the top of the abbey, you'll be rewarded with breathtaking panoramic views of the surrounding bay, where the interplay between tides and sand creates a natural spectacle. Make sure to check the tide times, as the island can be both accessible and isolated depending on the ebb and flow of the sea.

Saint-Malo Ramparts

Our next historical gem is the fortified city of Saint-Malo, a haven for history enthusiasts and adventurers alike. Encircled by mighty ramparts, this coastal town exudes a timeless charm, transporting visitors back to the era of privateers and corsairs.

Copyrighted Material © 123

Begin your exploration of Saint-Malo by strolling along the impressive ramparts. These stone walls, once designed to protect the town from invaders, now provide an extraordinary vantage point to admire the city's picturesque streets and stunning coastline. Let your imagination roam free as you envision the epic battles and maritime exploits that took place within these fortifications.

As you step into the heart of the city, you'll encounter an abundance of historic sites and architectural wonders. Pay a visit to the Saint-Malo Cathedral, a testament to Gothic and Romanesque styles with its striking spire and intricate stained glass. Explore the medieval Château de Saint-Malo, which houses a museum dedicated to the city's maritime heritage, allowing you to delve into its fascinating past.

Wander through the cobbled streets of the intra-muros, the historic center of

Copyrighted Material © 124

Saint-Malo, where you'll find an array of charming boutiques, art galleries, and seafood restaurants. Don't miss the chance to taste the region's culinary delights, especially the freshly caught seafood dishes that have become a hallmark of Breton cuisine.

For an extra dose of history, venture outside the city walls to the Solidor Tower and the National Fort of Saint-Père. These imposing structures provide insights into Saint-Malo's military past and offer captivating views of the Rance Estuary.

Carnac Megaliths

Our final destination in this historical odyssey takes us to the enigmatic Carnac Megaliths, a site shrouded in mystery and wonder. Located on the southern coast of Brittany, the Carnac Megaliths are one of the world's most extensive collections of prehistoric standing stones.

Copyrighted Material © 125

Prepare to be awe-struck as you enter this sprawling complex, spanning over four kilometers. The Carnac Megaliths are divided into three main alignments: the Ménec, Kermario, and Kerlescan alignments. These rows of towering stones, some reaching up to six meters in height, are arranged in precise patterns that have baffled archaeologists for centuries.

Take your time to explore each alignment, marveling at the sheer scale of the stones and pondering the purpose behind their construction. While the true meaning of the Carnac Megaliths remains elusive, theories suggest they were erected for religious, astronomical, or ceremonial purposes.

To gain further insights into this ancient civilization, visit the Museum of Prehistory in Carnac. Here, you'll find an extensive collection of artifacts, interactive exhibits, and informative displays that shed light on the lives and customs of the Neolithic people who erected these megaliths.

As you wander among these silent sentinels, let your imagination roam and contemplate the mysteries that surround them. The Carnac Megaliths stand as a testament to the ingenuity and spiritual beliefs of our ancestors, and their presence is a powerful reminder of the enduring legacy of human history.

While exploring these remarkable historical sites, let your senses absorb the stories etched into their walls, immerse yourself in their timeless charm, and embrace the profound connection between the present and the past.

Brittany's historical treasures await your discovery. Embark on this extraordinary adventure and create memories that will last a lifetime. Safe travels and may your journey

Copyrighted Material © 127

through Brittany's history be truly unforgettable!

B. Natural Wonders

As you embark on your journey through Brittany, France, get ready to immerse yourself in a world of breathtaking natural wonders. From windswept cliffs to serene coastlines, this region is a haven for nature enthusiasts seeking awe-inspiring landscapes. In this guide, we will explore three of Brittany's most captivating natural wonders: Pointe du Raz, Gulf of Morbihan, and Pink Granite Coast. So fasten your seatbelts and prepare to be captivated by the untouched beauty of this enchanting region.

Pointe du Raz: Where Land Meets The Roaring Atlantic

Located on the westernmost tip of France, Pointe du Raz is a mesmerizing headland

Copyrighted Material © 128

that marks the meeting point of land and the mighty Atlantic Ocean. It's often referred to as the "End of the World" due to its dramatic cliffs, wild winds, and crashing waves. As you stand at this precipice, you'll be overwhelmed by the sheer power and immensity of the ocean before you.

Nature enthusiasts will revel in the abundant birdlife that thrives in this rugged coastal environment. Keep an eye out for seabirds such as puffins, gannets, and razorbills, as they swoop and dive above the tumultuous waves. The bird observatory at Pointe du Raz offers a unique opportunity to learn more about these remarkable creatures and their natural habitats.

Take a leisurely hike along the well-marked coastal paths and be rewarded with panoramic views of the jagged cliffs and rocky islets that dot the shoreline. Capture the perfect photograph of the iconic Phare

Copyrighted Material © 129

de la Vieille lighthouse, standing stoically against the fierce elements.

Gulf of Morbihan: A Serene Haven of Tranquility

For those seeking a more peaceful natural wonder, the Gulf of Morbihan offers a serene and picturesque escape. This stunning inland sea, dotted with numerous islands, will transport you to a world of tranquility and natural beauty.

Embark on a boat trip and let the gentle breeze guide you through the labyrinthine network of islets, each with its unique charm. Explore the enchanting Île aux Moines, known for its quaint villages and scenic coastal paths. Take a moment to appreciate the unspoiled beaches and crystal-clear waters that surround you, inviting you to dive in and cool off on a hot summer's day.

Copyrighted Material © 130

Nature lovers will relish the opportunity to spot a variety of wildlife that calls the Gulf of Morbihan home. Keep your eyes peeled for playful dolphins that occasionally grace these waters with their presence. Admire the elegant grace of herons as they glide above the marshes, and marvel at the colorful plumage of kingfishers as they dart through the reeds.

Pink Granite Coast: Nature's Masterpiece Carved in Stone

Prepare to be spellbound by the ethereal beauty of the Pink Granite Coast, a geological marvel unlike any other. Stretching from Perros-Guirec to Trébeurden, this coast is renowned for its mesmerizing pink-hued rock formations, sculpted by the relentless forces of nature over millions of years.

Wander along the Sentier des Douaniers, a coastal path that winds its way through this

Copyrighted Material © 131

natural wonderland, revealing stunning vistas at every turn. Marvel at the iconic rock formations, aptly named the "Chaos of Ploumanac'h," as they emerge from the emerald waters, their rosy tones illuminated by the golden rays of the sun.

Photography enthusiasts will be in their element here, as the ever-changing light paints the landscape in a myriad of hues throughout the day. Capture the enchanting beauty of the pink rocks against the backdrop of the azure sea, and create memories that will last a lifetime.

For a truly unique experience, consider taking a guided kayak tour along the Pink Granite Coast. Glide through narrow passages and hidden coves, marveling at the intricate patterns and textures of the granite cliffs rising majestically from the water. Paddle past secluded beaches, accessible only by water, and bask in the tranquility of this untouched paradise.

Copyrighted Material © 132

As you explore the Pink Granite Coast, you'll encounter a rich diversity of plant and animal life. Admire the resilience of the vegetation that clings to the rugged cliffs, adding a touch of greenery to the pink canvas. Keep an eye out for seabirds nesting on the cliffs, and if you're lucky, you may spot a seal basking on a nearby rock.

To truly appreciate the geological wonders of this coast, visit the Geological Interpretation Center in Trégastel. Here, you can delve deeper into the fascinating formation processes that have shaped the Pink Granite Coast over millions of years. Learn about the unique properties of the granite and gain a deeper understanding of the forces that have created such a remarkable landscape.

As you explore these natural wonders in Brittany, it's important to respect and preserve their pristine beauty. Follow designated paths and adhere to any guidelines or restrictions in place to protect fragile ecosystems. Remember to leave no trace, taking your memories and photographs with you, but leaving the landscape as you found it for future generations to enjoy.

So, potential travelers, embrace the untamed beauty of Brittany and let these natural wonders ignite your sense of adventure. Lose yourself in the vastness of the Atlantic, find serenity in the secluded islands of the Gulf of Morbihan, and be enchanted by the mystical allure of the Pink Granite Coast. Brittany's natural wonders are waiting to be discovered, and they promise an unforgettable journey into the heart of nature's magnificence.

C. Museums & Galleries

Copyrighted Material © 134

Welcome to the captivating region of Brittany, France, where a tapestry of history, art, and culture awaits your exploration. In this part, we will delve into three prominent museums and galleries that showcase the vibrant heritage of Brittany. From the Musée de Bretagne to the Musée des Beaux-Arts de Quimper and the Musée d'Art et d'Histoire de Saint-Brieuc, each institution offers a unique perspective on the region's rich past and artistic treasures. Join us on this immersive journey as we unravel the wonders of Brittany's cultural tapestry.

Musée de Bretagne

Located in the heart of Rennes, the Musée de Bretagne is a must-visit destination for anyone seeking to understand the essence of Brittany. This museum boasts an extensive collection that encapsulates the diverse facets of the region's history, society, and traditions.

Copyrighted Material © 135

Spread across multiple galleries, the Musée de Bretagne traces Brittany's evolution from its ancient Celtic roots to the present day. From archaeological artifacts to interactive exhibits, visitors can immerse themselves in the captivating narratives that shaped Brittany's identity.

The museum's permanent exhibition offers a comprehensive overview of Brittany's cultural heritage, including its folk traditions, language, and rural life. Engaging displays present the region's rich maritime history, showcasing the importance of fishing, shipbuilding, and trade.

Additionally, the Musée de Bretagne frequently hosts temporary exhibitions that delve deeper into specific themes, such as contemporary art, regional crafts, and social issues. These curated displays ensure that

Copyrighted Material © 136

each visit to the museum offers a fresh and thought-provoking experience.

Musée des Beaux-Arts de Quimper

Nestled in the enchanting city of Quimper, the Musée des Beaux-Arts is a treasure trove for art enthusiasts. Boasting an impressive collection spanning several centuries, this museum showcases the mastery of renowned artists from Brittany and beyond.

The museum's permanent collection is a testament to the region's rich artistic legacy. Visitors can marvel at an array of paintings, sculptures, and decorative arts, including works by the esteemed Pont-Aven School. This avant-garde movement, spearheaded by artists like Paul Gauguin and Émile Bernard, sought to capture the vibrant landscapes and rural life of Brittany.

Moreover, the Musée des Beaux-Arts presents a diverse range of artistic styles,

Copyrighted Material © 137

from traditional to contemporary. This juxtaposition offers a fascinating dialogue between the old and the new, allowing visitors to appreciate the evolution of artistic expression over time.

Beyond its permanent collection, the museum frequently hosts temporary exhibitions that feature artists of national and international acclaim. These dynamic displays ensure that visitors can continually discover fresh perspectives and engage with contemporary art movements.

Musée d'Art et d'Histoire de Saint-Brieuc

Situated in the captivating city of Saint-Brieuc, the Musée d'Art et d'Histoire beckons history enthusiasts and art aficionados alike. This multidisciplinary institution weaves together the threads of art and history, presenting a captivating narrative of Brittany's past.

Copyrighted Material © 138

The museum's historical section offers a fascinating journey through time, spanning from prehistoric times to the modern era. Visitors can explore archaeological artifacts, medieval treasures, and interactive displays that shed light on Brittany's rich heritage.

The art collection at the Musée d'Art et d'Histoire showcases a diverse range of artistic movements and mediums. From classic paintings to contemporary installations, the museum celebrates the creative spirit of Brittany and beyond. Works by regional artists, such as Mathurin Méheut and Gustave-Louis Jaulmes, take center stage, offering an intimate glimpse into the region's artistic landscape.

One of the highlights of the Musée d'Art et d'Histoire is its collection of Breton religious art. Elaborate sculptures, intricately carved wooden altarpieces, and exquisite religious paintings demonstrate the profound

Copyrighted Material © 139

influence of Christianity on the region's artistic production.

The museum also boasts a remarkable collection of decorative arts, including furniture, ceramics, and textiles. These exquisite pieces showcase the craftsmanship and artistic sensibilities prevalent in Brittany throughout the centuries. Visitors can admire intricate tapestries, delicate porcelain, and ornate furniture, gaining insight into the region's refined aesthetic traditions.

In addition to its permanent displays, the Musée d'Art et d'Histoire regularly organizes temporary exhibitions that explore specific themes or artistic movements. These exhibitions offer a fresh perspective on the intersection of art and history, inviting visitors to delve deeper into the cultural tapestry of Brittany.

Practical Information

Copyrighted Material © 140

Musée de Bretagne

★ Location: 10 Cours des Alliés, Rennes.

★ From Tuesday through Sunday, from 10 am to 6 pm, the museum is open.

★ Admission: Entry to the museum is free for permanent exhibitions. Admission to temporary exhibitions could be charged.

★ Guided tours: The museum offers guided tours in multiple languages, providing insightful commentary on the exhibits. Check the museum's website for tour schedules and availability.

Musée des Beaux-Arts de Quimper

★ Location: 40 Place Saint-Corentin, Quimper.

★ Tuesday through Sunday from 10 am to 6 pm are the museum's hours of operation.

★ Admission: There is an admission fee for the museum, with discounted rates available for students, seniors, and groups.

★ Guided tours: Guided tours are available upon request. Visitors can inquire at the museum's information desk for tour options and availability.

Musée d'Art et d'Histoire de Saint-Brieuc

★ Location: 5 Place du Chai, Saint-Brieuc.

★ The museum is open from Tuesday through Sunday from 10 am to 6 pm.

Copyrighted Material © 142

★ Admission: Entry to the museum is free for permanent exhibitions. There may be an entrance fee for temporary exhibitions.

★ Guided tours: Guided tours are available upon reservation. Visitors can contact the museum's reception for tour options and availability.

As you venture through the museums and galleries of Brittany, you will embark on a captivating journey through the region's rich cultural heritage. The Musée de Bretagne in Rennes, with its immersive exhibits, offers a comprehensive understanding of Brittany's history and traditions. In Quimper, the Musée des Beaux-Arts showcases the artistic brilliance of the region, presenting a diverse range of artworks that span centuries. Lastly, the Musée d'Art et d'Histoire in Saint-Brieuc weaves together the threads of art and history, inviting you to explore the multifaceted tapestry of Brittany's past.

Each museum offers a unique perspective and a wealth of experiences for travelers seeking to immerse themselves in the vibrant cultural fabric of Brittany. So, pack your curiosity and embark on an unforgettable journey through the museums and galleries of this enchanting region. From ancient artifacts to contemporary masterpieces, you will witness the captivating legacy of Brittany unfold before your eyes.

Copyrighted Material © 144

VI. Outdoor Activities

With its diverse landscapes, rugged coastlines, lush forests, and charming countryside, Brittany offers an abundance of outdoor adventures for nature enthusiasts.

A. Hiking & Nature Trails

If you're seeking an unforgettable experience amidst the great outdoors, look no further than the region's captivating hiking and nature trails. In this comprehensive guide, we will unveil the most remarkable trails Brittany has to offer, ensuring you make the most of your time in this picturesque region.

Sentier des Douaniers (Customs Officers' Path)

Embark on an awe-inspiring journey along the Sentier des Douaniers, also known as the Customs Officers' Path. This trail stretches over 2,000 kilometers, hugging Brittany's stunning coastline. The path is divided into multiple sections, each offering unique vistas and natural wonders. From dramatic cliffs to sandy coves and charming fishing villages, this trail showcases Brittany's rugged beauty at its finest. Be prepared for a moderate to challenging hike, as some sections feature steep ascents and descents. Don't forget your camera, as the panoramic views along this iconic trail are simply breathtaking.

Brocéliande Forest

Immerse yourself in the mythical realm of King Arthur and the Knights of the Round Table as you explore the enchanting Brocéliande Forest. Located in central Brittany, this ancient forest is steeped in

Copyrighted Material © 146

legends and folklore. Follow the marked trails that wind through moss-covered trees, tranquil ponds, and mysterious megalithic sites. The most famous trail, Val Sans Retour (Valley of No Return), takes you to a rocky valley where, according to legend, unfaithful lovers were forever trapped. This mystical forest promises an ethereal experience for hikers and nature enthusiasts alike.

Pink Granite Coast

Prepare to be mesmerized by the unique geological wonders of the Pink Granite Coast. Situated in northern Brittany, this captivating stretch of coastline is renowned for its striking pink-hued rock formations. The Sentier des Douaniers also traverses this region, allowing you to discover the breathtaking landscapes up close. Marvel at the picturesque beaches, hidden coves, and massive boulders sculpted by wind and sea. The coastal path offers stunning panoramic

Copyrighted Material © 147

views, making it a paradise for photography enthusiasts. As you hike along this trail, take your time to appreciate the intricate beauty of nature's artwork.

Monts d'Arrée

For those seeking a rugged and untamed hiking experience, the Monts d'Arrée mountain range is a must-visit destination. Located in western Brittany, these ancient mountains provide a unique landscape that contrasts with the region's coastal beauty. The trails wind through heather-clad moorlands, granite outcrops, and pristine lakes, offering a sense of wilderness and tranquility. Mount Saint-Michel de Brasparts, the highest peak in Brittany, presents an excellent challenge for avid hikers. Be sure to pack appropriate gear and supplies, as the weather can be unpredictable in these higher altitudes.

Gulf of Morbihan

Copyrighted Material ©

Discover the natural wonders of the Gulf of Morbihan, a stunning inland sea dotted with numerous islands and islets. This area boasts an intricate network of trails that wind through coastal paths, salt marshes, and ancient forests. The Sentier des Douaniers follows the Gulf's shores, granting panoramic views of the turquoise waters and picturesque landscapes. Explore the charming islands of Île-aux-Moines and Île d'Arzon, each offering its unique charm and opportunities for hiking and exploration. Don't miss the opportunity to witness the spectacle of the tidal phenomenon known as "le mascaret," where a wave travels up the river, creating a thrilling natural spectacle. The Gulf of Morbihan is a true haven for nature lovers, offering a diverse range of flora and fauna, making it a paradise for birdwatching enthusiasts.

Armorique Regional Natural Park

Immerse yourself in the untouched beauty of the Armorique Regional Natural Park, a vast protected area covering over 125,000 hectares. Located in western Brittany, this park is a haven for outdoor enthusiasts, offering an array of hiking trails amidst diverse landscapes. Explore dense forests, picturesque lakes, cascading waterfalls, and rolling hills. The park is home to a rich variety of wildlife, including deer, otters, and numerous bird species. Whether you opt for a stroll or a challenging hike, the Armorique Regional Natural Park promises an unforgettable journey through unspoiled nature.

Odet River Valley

Indulge in the serenity and beauty of the Odet River Valley, a picturesque area that winds its way through lush green landscapes. This enchanting valley is known for its peaceful ambiance, charming villages,

Copyrighted Material © 150

and panoramic views. Follow the riverside trails as they meander through ancient forests, flower-filled meadows, and historic landmarks. Discover the stunning Château de Keriolet and the quaint town of Quimper, famous for its traditional pottery. The Odet River Valley offers a gentle and idyllic hiking experience, perfect for those seeking tranquility and natural splendor.

Pointe du Raz

Venture to the westernmost point of mainland France and experience the dramatic beauty of Pointe du Raz. This rugged headland, situated in Finistère, showcases the raw power of the Atlantic Ocean as it crashes against the cliffs. Hike along the marked trails that lead to breathtaking viewpoints, where you can marvel at the wild waves and soaring seabirds. Explore the coastal paths, ancient lighthouses, and hidden beaches. Pointe du Raz is a place of awe-inspiring beauty, offering a chance to connect with the untamed forces of nature.

Brittany's hiking and nature trails invite you to embark on a journey of discovery through its diverse landscapes and natural wonders. From the majestic coastline to ancient forests, from picturesque valleys to rugged mountains, each trail offers a unique experience that will leave you captivated and inspired. Whether you're a seasoned hiker or a nature enthusiast seeking serenity, Brittany has something to offer everyone. So lace up your hiking boots, breathe in the fresh air, and let the beauty of this remarkable region envelop you as you explore its magnificent trails.

B. Watersports & Beaches

Known for its rugged coastline, breathtaking landscapes, and vibrant culture, Brittany offers a plethora of exciting water sports activities and pristine beaches that cater to all kinds of travelers. Whether you're a thrill-seeker looking for an adrenaline rush or a leisurely beach lover seeking relaxation, Brittany has something for everyone. In this guide, we will explore the top watersports and beaches that make Brittany a haven for aquatic adventures. Get ready to dive into crystal-clear waters, ride the waves, and soak up the sun on stunning sandy shores!

Watersports in Brittany

Surfing in Quiberon

Quiberon, located on the Quiberon Peninsula, is a surfer's paradise boasting incredible waves and ideal wind conditions. Its consistent swell and wide sandy beaches attract surfers from all over the world. Whether you're a beginner or an experienced surfer, Quiberon offers surf schools and rental facilities to cater to all skill levels. Don't miss the iconic surf spot,

Copyrighted Material © 153

La Côte Sauvage, known for its powerful waves and breathtaking beauty. With its unique blend of adventure and natural splendor, surfing in Quiberon is an experience you won't want to miss.

Kiteboarding in Saint-Malo

Saint-Malo, a historic walled city on the Emerald Coast, is a hotspot for kiteboarding enthusiasts. The combination of strong coastal winds, vast sandy beaches, and stunning scenery make it an ideal location for this exhilarating sport. Novices can take lessons from experienced instructors, while experienced riders can enjoy the thrill of riding the waves and soaring through the air. The picturesque beaches of Saint-Malo, such as Sillon Beach and Bon Secours Beach, provide ample space to launch and land your kite, ensuring a memorable kiteboarding experience.

Kayaking in the Gulf of Morbihan

The Gulf of Morbihan, a stunning natural harbor dotted with small islands, is a kayaker's dream. Glide through calm turquoise waters, explore hidden coves, and discover the beauty of this unique marine environment. With numerous kayak rental services available, you can embark on guided tours or set off on your adventure. Visit the Île aux Moines, the largest island in the gulf, and be captivated by its unspoiled beaches and charming villages. Kayaking in the Gulf of Morbihan offers a peaceful escape and an opportunity to connect with nature.

Windsurfing in Carnac

Carnac, famous for its prehistoric standing stones, also offers excellent conditions for windsurfing. Its long sandy beaches and consistent winds attract windsurfing enthusiasts from around the world. Whether you're a beginner or an expert, you'll find rental shops and schools to suit your needs. The Bay of Quiberon, with its shallow waters and gentle waves, provides an ideal learning environment for beginners, while experienced windsurfers can venture farther into the bay for more challenging conditions. Experience the thrill of windsurfing in Carnac and witness the stunning megalithic monuments that dot the coastline.

Beaches in Brittany

Plage de l'Île Vierge, Crozon

Plage de l'Île Vierge, located in Crozon, is a hidden gem nestled within rugged cliffs and lush vegetation. Its turquoise waters, fine white sand, and tranquil atmosphere make it a perfect escape for those seeking peace and tranquility. Surrounded by unspoiled nature, this beach offers stunning panoramic views of the coastline. Take a stroll along the shore, bask in the sun, or

Copyrighted Material © 156

explore the nearby coastal paths for a memorable day in nature.

Plage de l'Ecluse, Dinard

Plage de l'Ecluse, situated in the charming town of Dinard, is a delightful family-friendly beach. With its soft sand and shallow waters, it's an ideal spot for sunbathing, building sandcastles, and swimming. The beach is well-equipped with facilities, including restaurants, cafes, and water sports equipment rentals. While here, don't miss the opportunity to explore the picturesque town of Dinard, known for its belle époque architecture and vibrant atmosphere.

Plage de la Grande Plage, Quiberon

Plage de la Grande Plage, located in the heart of Quiberon, is a popular beach renowned for its long stretch of fine sand and clear blue waters. This lively beach

Copyrighted Material © 157

offers a range of amenities, including beachfront restaurants, water sports rentals, and beach clubs. Whether you're looking to sunbathe, swim, or try your hand at various water sports, Plage de la Grande Plage has something for everyone.

Plage de l'Ériz, Belle-Île-en-Mer

Belle-Île-en-Mer, the largest of Brittany's islands, is home to Plage de l'Ériz. This picturesque beach captivates visitors with its dramatic cliffs, golden sand, and crystal-clear waters. Surrounded by breathtaking landscapes, Plage de l'Ériz is a paradise for nature lovers. Take a refreshing dip in the Atlantic Ocean, explore the nearby hiking trails, or simply unwind on the sandy shores while soaking in the island's beauty.

Plage de Trestraou, Perros-Guirec

Plage de Trestraou, located in the charming town of Perros-Guirec, is a captivating beach known for its pink granite rocks and picturesque views. Its fine sand and turquoise waters make it a haven for beachgoers. Take a stroll along the coast, enjoy a beachside picnic, or explore the stunning rock formations nearby. Don't forget to visit the Sentier des Douaniers (Customs Officers' Path), a scenic coastal trail that offers panoramic views of the rugged coastline.

Brittany's watersports and beaches offer a wealth of opportunities for adventure and relaxation. From riding the waves in Quiberon to kayaking in the Gulf of Morbihan, there's no shortage of thrilling activities to enjoy. And when it's time to unwind, the region's pristine beaches, such as Plage de l'Île Vierge and Plage de l'Ecluse, provide the perfect setting to soak up the sun and enjoy the beauty of nature. Plan your trip to Brittany, and discover a world of aquatic wonders, stunning landscapes, and unforgettable moments along the

Copyrighted Material © 159

enchanting coastline. Get ready to create memories that will last a lifetime in this breathtaking coastal haven.

C. Cycling & Bike Routes

This guide is designed for avid cyclists seeking an unforgettable adventure through Brittany's stunning landscapes. In this part, we will explore the region's top cycling routes, providing you with all the information you need to plan your cycling escapade in Brittany. From coastal paths to inland trails, prepare to immerse yourself in Brittany's natural beauty and discover the hidden gems that await you at every turn of the pedal.

The Pink Granite Coast

Our journey begins along the enchanting Pink Granite Coast, a stretch of shoreline adorned with captivating rock formations.

Copyrighted Material © 160

Start your ride in Perros-Guirec and follow the coastal route towards Ploumanac'h, where you'll witness the unique fusion of pink granite and azure waters. As you pedal along, take in the breathtaking vistas of the Côte de Granit Rose, and be sure to make a stop at the stunning Ploumanac'h lighthouse. With its awe-inspiring scenery and smooth cycling paths, this route is perfect for riders of all skill levels.

The Gulf of Morbihan

Next, venture south to explore the Gulf of Morbihan, a true gem in Brittany's cycling crown. Begin your journey in Vannes and wind your way around the gulf, passing through quaint fishing villages and ancient sites. Pedal along the Vannes-Arradon Greenway for a peaceful ride, or challenge yourself with the Circuit des Alignements, a longer route offering a glimpse into Brittany's prehistoric past. Keep your camera ready to capture the gulf's

Copyrighted Material © 161

ever-changing landscapes and stunning seascapes.

Belle-Île-en-Mer

For an island adventure, head to Belle-Île-en-Mer, Brittany's largest island, and a cyclist's paradise. Start your exploration in Le Palais and embark on the island's circuit, encircling its rugged coastline. Prepare to be amazed by the dramatic cliffs, sandy coves, and picturesque harbors that make Belle-Île-en-Mer a true haven for nature enthusiasts. The circuit offers varying difficulty levels, allowing riders to choose between leisurely coastal paths or challenging mountainous terrain. Don't miss the opportunity to visit the charming villages of Sauzon and Bangor along the way.

The Nantes-Brest Canal

For a tranquil cycling experience, the Nantes-Brest Canal route is a must-ride. Stretching across 364 kilometers, this historic canal offers a flat and well-maintained trail that meanders through lush countryside and charming villages. Begin your journey in Nantes or Brest and pedal along the towpath, encountering picturesque locks, stone bridges, and peaceful waterways. This route is perfect for those seeking a leisurely ride, with plenty of opportunities to immerse yourself in the region's rural beauty and enjoy local gastronomic delights.

The Armorique Regional Natural Park

Our cycling odyssey continues in the Armorique Regional Natural Park, a haven for nature enthusiasts and outdoor adventurers. Start in Ploudalmézeau and explore the park's diverse landscapes, including rugged cliffs, pristine beaches, and rolling hills. The park offers an extensive network of cycling trails, allowing riders to tailor their route based on preferences and skill levels. As you pedal through the park, keep an eye out for the unique flora and fauna that call this region home.

The Monts d'Arrée

Conclude your Brittany cycling adventure in the Monts d'Arrée, a mountain range known for its untamed beauty and mythical allure. Begin in Huelgoat and traverse the range's winding roads and rugged paths, surrounded by enchanting forests and ancient legends. For a challenging ride, tackle the famous Roc'h Ruz climb, which rewards you with panoramic views from the summit. The Monts d'Arrée offers a truly immersive experience for cyclists, where you can reconnect with nature and embrace the region's rich folklore.

Congratulations on reaching the end of our cycling journey through Brittany! From the

Copyrighted Material © 164

mesmerizing Pink Granite Coast to the mythical Monts d'Arrée, this region offers a wealth of cycling opportunities for every adventurer. As you plan your trip, remember to pack essentials like a reliable bike, safety gear, and plenty of water. So, gear up, get ready to pedal, and embark on an unforgettable cycling adventure in beautiful Brittany!

D. Golf Courses

Welcome, avid golf enthusiasts, to the enchanting region of Brittany, France! Renowned for its picturesque landscapes, rich cultural heritage, and delectable cuisine, Brittany also boasts some of Europe's finest golf courses. In this comprehensive guide, we will explore the exquisite golfing destinations that await you in this captivating region. From coastal gems to inland wonders, Brittany's golf courses offer a harmonious blend of natural beauty and exceptional gameplay. Prepare to immerse yourself in the lush fairways, challenging bunkers, and panoramic views that make these courses an absolute delight. Whether you are a seasoned golfer or a leisurely player seeking a memorable experience, Brittany's golf courses are sure to exceed your expectations.

Golf Blue Green Pléneuf-Val-André

Located on the breathtaking Emerald Coast, Golf Blue Green Pléneuf-Val-André is a golfer's paradise. This 18-hole championship course, designed by Alain Prat, offers a perfect blend of challenging holes and stunning coastal vistas. The fairways wind their way through lush greenery, while the strategically placed bunkers and water hazards add an element of excitement to the game. Golfers of all skill levels can enjoy the course, thanks to its multiple tee options. After a rewarding round, indulge in a well-deserved meal at

Copyrighted Material © 166

the clubhouse, overlooking the shimmering waters of the English Channel. With its idyllic setting and impeccable maintenance, Golf Blue Green Pléneuf-Val-André guarantees an unforgettable golfing experience.

Golf de Dinard

Nestled on the emerald cliffs overlooking the English Channel, Golf de Dinard is a historic gem that has been enticing golfers since 1887. This iconic course, designed by Tom Dunn and Willie Park Jr., seamlessly combines challenging holes with breathtaking views. With its undulating fairways, strategically positioned bunkers, and fast greens, Golf de Dinard offers an exhilarating test of skill. The course's coastal location not only provides stunning vistas but also poses a thrilling challenge with the ever-present sea breeze. After an invigorating round, bask in the elegance of the clubhouse, which exudes a timeless charm reminiscent of the Belle Époque era. Golf de Dinard is a must-visit destination for golfers seeking a harmonious blend of history, natural beauty, and exceptional gameplay.

Golf Blue Green Rennes Saint-Jacques

Nestled in the heart of Brittany, Golf Blue Green Rennes Saint-Jacques presents an idyllic retreat for golfers. This picturesque 27-hole course, designed by Robert Berthet, harmoniously merges with the region's tranquil landscapes. Set amidst ancient woodlands, the course offers a peaceful ambiance as you navigate its challenging fairways and greens. The cleverly placed water hazards and well-guarded bunkers demand precision and strategic play. Golf Blue Green Rennes Saint-Jacques also features a state-of-the-art practice facility, allowing players to hone their skills before tackling the course. Immerse yourself in the

Copyrighted Material © 168

natural splendor of Brittany while indulging in a memorable golfing experience at this hidden gem.

Golf de Cornouaille

Tucked away on the southern coast of Brittany, Golf de Cornouaille is a true hidden gem. This remarkable 18-hole course, designed by Fred and Martin Hawtree, showcases the region's rugged beauty and maritime charm. The fairways wind through a diverse landscape of dunes, heather-covered hills, and ancient oak trees, providing a captivating visual experience. Golf de Cornouaille's layout offers a balanced mix of challenges, with strategic bunkering and undulating greens testing golfers' skills. The breathtaking views of the Atlantic Ocean add an extra touch of magic to the game. After an exhilarating round, savor a meal at the clubhouse, where you can relish the panoramic vistas of the course and the mesmerizing coastline.

Copyrighted Material © 169

Golf de Saint-Malo

Situated near the historic city of Saint-Malo, Golf de Saint-Malo offers a remarkable golfing experience steeped in natural beauty. This 27-hole course, designed by Hubert Chesneau, features a stunning blend of woodland and coastal scenery. With its undulating fairways, numerous water hazards, and strategic bunkers, the course demands precision and strategic play. Golfers will find themselves captivated by the breathtaking views of Mont Saint-Michel Bay, adding an unforgettable element to their game. The clubhouse's warm ambiance provides the perfect setting to relax and recount the day's highlights. Golf de Saint-Malo is a haven for golfers seeking an unforgettable fusion of challenging play and stunning vistas.

Embrace the synergy of golf and travel, as Brittany reveals its secrets through the

Copyrighted Material © 170

artistry of its golf courses. Now, it's time to pack your clubs, prepare for an adventure, and create lasting memories on the fairways of Brittany. Bon voyage and may your golfing escapades be nothing short of extraordinary!

E. Fishing & Boating

With its diverse coastline, serene rivers, and pristine lakes, Brittany offers an idyllic setting for fishing and boating enthusiasts. Whether you seek the thrill of deep-sea fishing, the tranquility of freshwater angling, or the joy of sailing along the stunning coastline, Brittany has it all. Join us as we embark on a journey through the region's abundant fishing spots, navigable waterways, and boating opportunities, ensuring an unforgettable experience for every traveler seeking aquatic adventures.

Fishing in Brittany

Copyrighted Material © 171

Coastal Fishing

Brittany's vast coastline, stretching over 2,800 kilometers, provides ample opportunities for coastal fishing enthusiasts. The region boasts a rich marine ecosystem, making it a haven for both recreational and professional fishermen. Charter a fishing boat and set sail from one of the many coastal towns, such as Concarneau or Saint-Malo, to explore the bountiful waters of the English Channel and the Atlantic Ocean.

Within these marine waters, you'll find a wide variety of fish species, including cod, sea bass, mackerel, and plaice. Cast your line and feel the excitement as you reel in your catch, surrounded by breathtaking coastal scenery. Local fishing charters and experienced guides can help you navigate the best spots, share insider knowledge, and ensure a successful fishing expedition.

Copyrighted Material © 172

Inland Fishing

Brittany's picturesque lakes, rivers, and streams offer a peaceful retreat for freshwater fishing enthusiasts. The region is home to countless pristine water bodies, including the Lac de Guerlédan, the Vilaine River, and the Nantes-Brest Canal. These tranquil spots are teeming with fish, presenting an opportunity to engage in angling amidst beautiful natural surroundings.

Whether you prefer fly fishing, spinning, or coarse fishing, Brittany's inland waters cater to all fishing techniques. Here, you can target species such as trout, pike, perch, and carp. Seek advice from local fishing clubs or hire a knowledgeable fishing guide to discover the best locations, learn about local regulations, and increase your chances of making a memorable catch.

Copyrighted Material © 173

Fishing Events & Festivals

Brittany's deep-rooted fishing culture is celebrated through various events and festivals that showcase the region's maritime traditions. One such event is the Fête de la Mer (Sea Festival), which takes place annually in ports and fishing villages across Brittany. Enjoy lively parades, maritime exhibitions, and mouthwatering seafood tastings while immersing yourself in the vibrant coastal atmosphere.

For avid anglers, Brittany hosts several fishing competitions throughout the year, offering an exciting opportunity to test your skills and compete with fellow enthusiasts. The popular "Fishing at Dawn" event attracts participants from all over Europe, who gather to showcase their fishing prowess and enjoy a friendly competition in Brittany's abundant waters.

Boating Adventures in Brittany

Sailing & Yachting

The stunning Brittany coastline is a paradise for sailing enthusiasts, with its rugged cliffs, hidden coves, and picturesque islands. Charter a sailboat or yacht and embark on a remarkable maritime journey, exploring the diverse archipelagos of Brittany, such as the Glénan Islands or the Gulf of Morbihan.

Whether you're an experienced sailor or a novice, Brittany offers suitable sailing conditions for all skill levels. Set sail on the calm waters of sheltered bays or venture into the open sea for an exhilarating adventure. Moor your vessel at charming harbors and coastal towns, where you can experience the unique maritime heritage of Brittany and indulge in delectable seafood cuisine.

Canal & River Cruising

Inland waterways, including canals and rivers, present an alternative and serene way to explore Brittany's enchanting landscapes. The Nantes-Brest Canal and the Vilaine River offer navigable routes, allowing boaters to leisurely cruise through the region's diverse countryside.

Rent a canal boat or river cruiser and meander along these tranquil waterways, passing through picturesque villages, lush vineyards, and verdant forests. Experience the charm of lock systems as you traverse the canals, allowing for a truly immersive boating experience in the heart of Brittany's rural beauty.

Watersports & Kayaking

For thrill-seekers and adventure enthusiasts, Brittany's dynamic waters offer a wide range of exciting activities. Try your hand at kayaking along the rugged coastline, navigating through sea caves, and exploring

Copyrighted Material © 176

hidden coves. Feel the adrenaline rush as you ride the waves while windsurfing or kitesurfing in Brittany's wind-rich spots, such as Douarnenez Bay or La Torche.

If you prefer a more relaxed watersport, paddleboarding is a fantastic option, allowing you to admire the region's stunning coastal panoramas at your own pace. Additionally, Brittany's rivers and lakes provide excellent conditions for canoeing and kayaking, granting access to hidden corners of natural beauty.

Practical Tips

Fishing & Boating Regulations

Before embarking on your fishing or boating adventure in Brittany, familiarize yourself with the local regulations. Obtain the necessary permits, licenses, and adhere to size and catch limits to ensure responsible angling. Familiarize yourself with

Copyrighted Material © 177

navigational rules, safety equipment requirements, and local weather conditions for a safe and enjoyable boating experience.

Best Time to Visit

Brittany's fishing and boating seasons vary throughout the year. Coastal fishing is best during spring and summer when fish species are abundant, while inland fishing can be enjoyed year-round. Boating is popular from May to September when the weather is mild and the sea conditions are favorable. Plan your visit accordingly to maximize your chances of a successful and enjoyable fishing or boating trip.

Immerse yourself in the region's natural beauty, partake in fishing events and festivals, and explore the diverse waterways that make this destination a haven for aquatic pursuits. Come, cast your line, set sail, and create memories that will last a

Copyrighted Material © 178

lifetime in the enchanting waters of Brittany.

VII. Local Cuisine & Dining

With its rich cultural heritage, breathtaking landscapes, and, of course, its delectable cuisine, Brittany offers a truly unforgettable culinary experience. In this chapter, we will embark on a gastronomic journey, exploring the unique local flavors, traditional dishes,

Copyrighted Material © 179

and dining customs that make Brittany a paradise for food enthusiasts.

A. Traditional Breton Dishes

This guide will take you on a culinary adventure, unveiling the secrets of traditional Breton dishes. From hearty seafood delicacies to mouthwatering crepes, prepare your taste buds for a remarkable journey through the vibrant flavors of Brittany.

Galettes: The Soul of Breton Cuisine

Origins & Characteristics

Breton cuisine is incomplete without mentioning its iconic dish, the galette. This savory buckwheat crepe is a staple food that has been enjoyed in Brittany for centuries. Galettes have a distinctive nutty flavor and a

Copyrighted Material © 180

slightly crisp texture, making them a perfect vessel for various fillings.

Popular Fillings

★ Complete Galette: The most traditional and beloved filling comprises ham, Emmental cheese, and a perfectly cooked egg. The combination of flavors and textures in this classic galette is truly irresistible.

★ Galette Complète Forestière: For mushroom enthusiasts, this variation includes a generous serving of sautéed mushrooms, complemented by melted cheese and a sunny-side-up egg.

★ Galette Saucisse: This popular street food option features a grilled Breton sausage, encased in a warm galette, creating a delightful and satisfying snack.

Copyrighted Material © 181

Seafood Delicacies: A Bountiful Coastal Feast

With its extensive coastline, Brittany offers an abundance of fresh seafood. Indulge in the region's maritime treasures, prepared using traditional cooking techniques that have been passed down through generations.

Moules Marinières: A Coastal Classic

Brittany's Moules Marinières is a dish that showcases the simple yet exquisite flavors of the sea. Fresh mussels are steamed in a flavorful broth of white wine, shallots, garlic, and parsley, resulting in a tantalizing aroma and a taste that transports you to the seashore.

Coquilles Saint-Jacques: Scallops Refined

Brittany is renowned for its succulent scallops, known locally as Coquilles

Copyrighted Material © 182

Saint-Jacques. This delicacy is often pan-seared to achieve a golden crust while retaining its tender texture. Served with a velvety sauce, such as beurre blanc or a creamy mushroom sauce, Coquilles Saint-Jacques is a culinary delight.

Homard à l'Armoricaine: Lobster Extravaganza

Indulge in the ultimate seafood feast with Homard à l'Armoricaine. This hearty dish features lobster cooked in a rich tomato-based sauce, infused with brandy and a hint of saffron. A symphony of tastes emerges as a result, leaving you wanting more.

Cotriade: A Rustic Fish Stew

Embark on a culinary journey with Cotriade, a traditional Breton fish stew. Prepared with a medley of locally caught fish, potatoes, onions, and aromatic herbs, this hearty dish

Copyrighted Material © 183

is a celebration of coastal flavors. Cotriade is best enjoyed with a crusty baguette to soak up the delectable broth.

Crêpes: Sweet & Savory Delights

No exploration of Breton cuisine is complete without savoring its world-famous crêpes. From delightful street food to elegant desserts, crêpes offer a wide range of flavors to satisfy every palate.

Crêpes de Froment: A Sweet Symphony

Made from wheat flour, Crêpes de Froment are the quintessential sweet crepes. Whether enjoyed with a simple sprinkle of sugar and a squeeze of lemon or topped with decadent Nutella or salted caramel, these thin and delicate delights are a true gastronomic pleasure.

Galette de Sarrasin: Savory Sensations

Copyrighted Material © 184

Distinct from the galette mentioned earlier, Galette de Sarrasin is a savory buckwheat crepe that serves as a canvas for a myriad of fillings. From traditional combinations like ham, cheese, and egg to inventive creations featuring smoked salmon, goat cheese, and caramelized onions, the possibilities are endless.

Kouign-Amann: Buttery Bliss

Indulge in the rich and buttery goodness of Kouign-Amann, a traditional Breton pastry. This flaky, caramelized delight is made with layers of butter and sugar, resulting in a heavenly treat that pairs perfectly with a cup of coffee.

Cidre: Brittany's Traditional Beverage

To complement the delectable flavors of Breton cuisine, immerse yourself in the region's traditional beverage—cidre. Brittany is renowned for its apple orchards

Copyrighted Material © 185

and the art of cider-making, resulting in a wide variety of flavors and styles.

Types of Cidre

★ Cidre Doux: With its natural sweetness, Cidre Doux is a perfect introduction to Breton cider. The low alcohol content and fruity profile make it a refreshing choice for a sunny afternoon.

★ Cidre Brut: For those seeking a drier and more robust cider, Cidre Brut is the ideal choice. With a higher alcohol content and a crisp, tart flavor, it pairs well with savory dishes and cheeses.

★ Cidrerie Visits: Explore the picturesque cidreries scattered across the region, where you can witness the cider-making process firsthand. Engage with local producers, sample different varieties, and gain insights into the cultural significance of cider in Brittany.

Embark on a gastronomic journey through Brittany, where traditional Breton dishes tantalize the senses and showcase the region's rich culinary heritage. From the iconic galettes to the bountiful seafood delicacies and delectable crêpes, each bite reveals the passion and craftsmanship of Breton cuisine. So, immerse yourself in the vibrant flavors, explore the coastal treasures, and savor the timeless traditions that make Brittany a paradise for food lovers. Bon appétit!

B. Popular Restaurants & Cafés

In this guide, we will delve into the diverse and vibrant restaurant and café scene of Brittany, showcasing the most popular establishments that will take you on a gastronomic journey like no other.

Copyrighted Material © 187

Quaint Coastal Eateries

La Trinquette

Nestled in the picturesque town of Concarneau, La Trinquette is a charming coastal eatery that captures the essence of Brittany's maritime traditions. Specializing in fresh seafood, this restaurant offers a delightful array of dishes, including succulent oysters, flavorsome fish stews, and grilled lobster. With its cozy ambiance and stunning waterfront views, La Trinquette promises a memorable dining experience.

Le Petit Port

Located in the charming port town of Doëlan, Le Petit Port is a hidden gem adored by locals and visitors alike. Known for its warm hospitality and exquisite seafood, the restaurant serves up delicacies

Copyrighted Material © 188

like langoustines, scallops, and the regional specialty, "cotriade," a hearty fisherman's stew. Indulge in a delectable meal while gazing out at the idyllic harbor setting.

Le Café du Port

Situated on the quayside of the vibrant city of Saint-Malo, Le Café du Port offers a mix of traditional Breton cuisine and innovative flavors. With its nautical-themed décor, the restaurant exudes a cozy atmosphere. Don't miss out on their mouthwatering galettes (savory buckwheat crepes) and delectable seafood platters, accompanied by a glass of local cider.

Gastronomic Haunts in the City

Le Saint-James

Located in Bouliac, just outside of Bordeaux, Le Saint-James is an acclaimed restaurant helmed by Michelin-starred chef Nicolas

Copyrighted Material © 189

Magie. Offering panoramic views of the city, this culinary gem showcases innovative interpretations of classic dishes using local and seasonal ingredients. Indulge in the exquisite tasting menu and let your senses be enchanted.

L'Auberge Bretonne

Situated in the medieval town of La Roche-Bernard, L'Auberge Bretonne is a gastronomic haven renowned for its dedication to regional flavors. Chef Loïc Le Bail combines traditional techniques with contemporary creativity, resulting in dishes that celebrate the best of Brittany's culinary heritage. From delicate seafood preparations to flavorful meat dishes, every plate tells a story.

Le Comptoir de Saint-Malo

In the heart of Saint-Malo, Le Comptoir de Saint-Malo is a vibrant restaurant that

Copyrighted Material © 190

embodies the region's love for quality produce and convivial dining. This modern bistro offers a delectable menu featuring seasonal ingredients sourced from local producers. Be sure to savor their exquisite platters of fresh oysters and indulge in the classic Breton dessert, kouign-amann.

Quirky Cafés & Patisseries

Maison Georges Larnicol: Located in the heart of Quimper, Maison Georges Larnicol is a delightful patisserie that has been tantalizing taste buds since 1977. Known for its colorful displays of chocolates and mouth watering pastries, this family-owned establishment offers a wide selection of sweet treats, including the famous "kouignettes" (miniature kouign-amann) and delectable macarons.

La Maison du Kouign-Amann

Copyrighted Material © 191

A trip to Brittany would be incomplete without savoring the iconic kouign-amann. In Douarnenez, La Maison du Kouign-Amann is the ultimate destination for this buttery, caramelized pastry. Expert bakers create these delights using traditional techniques, ensuring a perfect balance of flakiness and sweetness in every bite.

Café du Marché

Tucked away in the charming town of Dinan, Café du Marché offers a cozy and laid-back atmosphere, making it the perfect spot to unwind with a cup of coffee or tea. Delight in their homemade cakes and pastries, or indulge in a leisurely brunch while soaking up the authentic Breton ambiance.

From quaint coastal eateries that highlight the region's maritime traditions to gastronomic havens that redefine classic dishes, Brittany's restaurant and café scene promise an unforgettable culinary adventure. Whether you're a seafood enthusiast, a lover of traditional Breton flavors, or a sweet tooth yearning for delectable pastries, the diverse range of establishments in Brittany will cater to your every craving. So, embark on a gastronomic journey through Brittany and savor the unique blend of history, culture, and exquisite flavors that this captivating region has to offer. Bon appétit!

VIII. Shopping & Souvenirs

As you embark on your journey through the picturesque region of Brittany, France, you'll undoubtedly come across a wealth of shopping opportunities and unique souvenirs that capture the essence of this beautiful destination. From charming local markets and crafts to artisanal boutiques, Brittany offers a delightful array of shopping experiences

A. Local Crafts & Artisans

One of the best ways to immerse yourself in the local culture is by exploring the unique crafts and artisans that call Brittany home. From intricate lacework to exquisite pottery, Brittany offers a treasure trove of traditional and contemporary artistry. In this chapter, we will take you on a journey through the fascinating world of Brittany's local crafts and artisans, highlighting their distinctive techniques, cultural significance, and where to find them.

Pottery & Ceramic Traditions

Brittany has a long-standing tradition of pottery and ceramic craftsmanship, with distinct styles and techniques found throughout the region. Artisans often draw inspiration from the surrounding natural beauty, resulting in pieces that reflect the rugged coastal landscapes and the vibrant colors of the sea.

Quimper Faience is one of the most renowned pottery styles in Brittany, originating from the town of Quimper. Recognizable by its hand-painted motifs featuring Breton figures in traditional costumes, Quimper Faience pieces make for wonderful souvenirs or decorative items for your home. Visit the Faïencerie Henriot-Quimper to witness the skilled artisans at work and browse their exquisite collections.

For those seeking a more contemporary twist on pottery, head to the village of La Poterie de la Reine in Locmariaquer. Here, you can find innovative ceramic pieces created by local artists, showcasing a fusion

Copyrighted Material © 195

of traditional craftsmanship and modern design.

Intricate Lacework

Lacework is an integral part of Brittany's cultural heritage, and the delicate artistry can be traced back centuries. The town of Pont-l'Abbé is particularly known for its lace-making traditions, with intricate designs and patterns adorning shawls, collars, and table linens.

To witness the creation of exquisite lacework firsthand, visit the Maison du Pays Bigouden in Pont-l'Abbé. This museum not only showcases a collection of historic lace pieces but also hosts demonstrations by skilled lace makers, offering visitors a glimpse into the meticulous craftsmanship involved.

Breton Textiles

Copyrighted Material © 196

Brittany's textile industry is renowned for its production of high-quality fabrics, with strong connections to the region's maritime heritage. The iconic striped Breton shirt, known as "marinière," is a classic example of Breton textiles and has become a symbol of French fashion.

To find authentic Breton textiles, make your way to the charming town of Quiberon. Here, you'll discover local boutiques such as Armor-Lux, known for their commitment to preserving the traditional craftsmanship of Breton textiles. From striped shirts to cozy woolen blankets, these boutiques offer a wide range of products that embody the spirit of Brittany.

Basketry & Wickerwork

Brittany's coastal landscapes and agricultural traditions have given rise to a thriving basketry and wickerwork industry. Local artisans skillfully weave natural

Copyrighted Material © 197

materials like willow and rush into functional and decorative objects, such as baskets, trays, and lampshades.

To witness the art of basket weaving, visit the Atelier de Vannerie in the town of Pont-Scorff. Here, you can explore the workshop, where talented craftsmen create beautiful baskets using traditional techniques. Don't forget to browse their showroom, where you can find a variety of woven creations to bring home as souvenirs.

Woodworking & Furniture

Brittany boasts a rich tradition of woodworking and furniture making, with artisans renowned for their craftsmanship and attention to detail. From intricately carved furniture to decorative wooden sculptures, the region offers a wealth of options for those seeking unique wooden creations.

The town of Dinan is a haven for woodworking enthusiasts, with numerous workshops and galleries showcasing the work of local artisans. Explore the charming streets lined with artisanal boutiques, such as L'Atelier d'Ébénisterie, to discover one-of-a-kind furniture pieces and handcrafted wooden objects.

Jewelry & Metalwork

Brittany's jewelry and metalwork industry is steeped in history and craftsmanship, producing stunning pieces that reflect the region's cultural heritage. Artisans skillfully incorporate traditional motifs, such as Celtic symbols and maritime themes, into their designs.

To find exquisite jewelry and metalwork, head to the city of Rennes, where you'll discover a vibrant artisan scene. Visit Les Ateliers du Temps, a collective of talented jewelers, to explore a diverse range of

Copyrighted Material © 199

handmade jewelry, including rings, earrings, and necklaces, crafted with precision and creativity.

Exploring Brittany's local crafts and artisans is a truly enriching experience, offering a deeper understanding of the region's culture and heritage. From pottery and lacework to textiles and woodworking, the skilled artisans of Brittany continue to preserve and innovate traditional craftsmanship. By supporting these local artists and bringing home their unique creations, you not only acquire a memorable souvenir but also contribute to the preservation of Brittany's rich artistic legacy. So, go ahead and embark on a journey through the enchanting world of Brittany's crafts and artisans – a journey that will leave you inspired and in awe of their incredible talent.

B. Markets & Flea Markets

Copyrighted Material © 200

We will delve into the heart of Brittany's market culture, highlighting its rich history, vibrant ambiance, and diverse offerings. From artisanal delights to vintage treasures, prepare to be enchanted by the unique shopping experiences that await you in Brittany's markets.

Brittany's Market Culture

Historical Significance

Brittany has a long-standing tradition of vibrant markets, dating back centuries. These markets were essential for locals to trade goods and connect with neighboring communities. Today, they serve as a testament to the region's cultural heritage.

Market Days

Markets are an integral part of Brittany's social fabric, with different towns and cities hosting their markets on specific days of the

Copyrighted Material © 201

week. This allows both residents and visitors to plan their itineraries accordingly, ensuring they don't miss out on the market experience.

Regional Products

Brittany's markets boast an extensive array of fresh, locally sourced produce. From colorful fruits and vegetables to seafood caught that morning, you'll find a cornucopia of culinary delights. Don't forget to try the renowned Brittany butter, cider, and galettes, a type of savory pancake.

Traditional Markets in Brittany

Rennes Market

Rennes, the capital city of Brittany, is home to a vibrant and sprawling market. Held every Saturday, it attracts vendors from across the region, offering a diverse range of products. From clothing and accessories to

Copyrighted Material © 202

household items and antiques, Rennes Market is a treasure trove for shopaholics.

Saint-Malo Market

Located on the coast, the charming city of Saint-Malo hosts a bustling market on Tuesdays and Fridays. Here, you'll find a delightful mix of fresh seafood, regional delicacies, and local crafts. The market's location near the picturesque beaches adds an extra touch of magic.

Quimper Market

Quimper, known for its traditional Breton pottery, boasts a remarkable market experience every Wednesday and Saturday. The market square buzzes with activity as vendors showcase their pottery alongside fresh local produce, textiles, and souvenirs. Don't miss the chance to admire the intricate craftsmanship of the Quimper pottery.

Copyrighted Material © 203

Vannes Market

Vannes, a medieval town brimming with history, welcomes visitors to its vibrant market on Wednesdays and Saturdays. Here, you'll discover a delightful blend of local produce, seafood, flowers, and regional specialties. As you explore the market, take a moment to explore the town's well-preserved medieval architecture.

Charming Flea Markets in Brittany

Lorient Flea Market

Lorient's flea market, held every first Saturday of the month, entices treasure hunters and vintage enthusiasts alike. Spanning across several streets, this market offers a plethora of antiques, second-hand goods, and curiosities. From retro fashion to unique home decor, you'll find hidden gems that carry stories of the past.

Copyrighted Material © 204

Brest Flea Market

Brest, a city with a rich maritime history, hosts a monthly flea market on Sundays. Here, you can browse through an eclectic mix of vintage furniture, vinyl records, collectibles, and more. The maritime theme adds a distinctive charm to this treasure trove of nostalgia.

Redon Flea Market

The historic town of Redon hosts a delightful flea market every third Sunday of the month. Nestled along the banks of the Vilaine River, this market offers an enchanting atmosphere and a wide range of antiques, books, and crafts. It's the perfect place to uncover unique souvenirs and one-of-a-kind finds.

Dinard Flea Market

Copyrighted Material © 205

Dinard, a coastal town renowned for its Belle Époque charm, holds a charming flea market during the summer months. Stroll along the promenade, adorned with stalls brimming with vintage clothing, antique jewelry, and trinkets from yesteryears. Enjoy the sea breeze as you hunt for treasures by the shore.

Tips for Exploring Brittany's Markets

1. Timing: Arrive early to soak up the vibrant atmosphere and secure the best finds. Locals often recommend going in the morning to experience the markets at their liveliest.

2. Haggling: Haggling is a common practice in flea markets, but less so in traditional markets. Remember to approach negotiations respectfully, always keeping in mind the value of the item and the vendor's expertise.

Copyrighted Material © 206

3. Payment: Carry sufficient cash as some vendors may not accept credit cards. Additionally, it's a good idea to have small denominations for convenience.

4. Respect Local Customs: Embrace the local customs and traditions while visiting markets. Engage with vendors, ask questions, and show appreciation for the regional products.

Brittany's markets and flea markets are a gateway to the region's vibrant culture and heritage. Whether you're seeking fresh produce, unique souvenirs, or a nostalgic trip through time, these markets have something for everyone. Immerse yourself in the bustling ambiance, savor the flavors, and embark on a shopping adventure that will leave you with cherished memories of Brittany's market treasures. Bon voyage!

Copyrighted Material © 207

C. Shopping Districts & Boutiques

Brittany is also home to a plethora of charming shopping districts and boutiques that are sure to captivate your senses. This guide will take you on a journey through the most noteworthy shopping destinations in the region, highlighting their unique offerings, local specialties, and must-visit boutiques. So, grab your walking shoes, and let's embark on an unforgettable shopping adventure in Brittany!

Rennes - Where Tradition Meets Modernity

Our first stop is the vibrant capital city of Brittany, Rennes. Combining medieval charm with a modern twist, Rennes offers a diverse range of shopping experiences. Start your exploration in the historic city center, where you'll find picturesque cobblestone streets lined with boutique shops and specialty stores. Rue Saint-Michel is a

Copyrighted Material © 208

must-visit, with its array of fashion boutiques and trendy concept stores.

For those seeking high-end fashion and luxury brands, head to Rue de la Monnaie, where you'll find upscale boutiques offering the latest collections from renowned designers. If you're a fan of local craftsmanship, make sure to visit Les Ateliers du Vent, an art and design space that showcases the works of talented local artists.

Food enthusiasts will be delighted by the Halles Centrales, a bustling covered market filled with stalls brimming with fresh produce, local cheeses, seafood, and more. Indulge in authentic Breton specialties like galettes (buckwheat crepes) and cider, which you can purchase from the market or enjoy at one of the charming cafes nearby.

Quimper - A Ceramic Wonderland

Next on our shopping itinerary is Quimper, a town renowned for its exquisite faience pottery. Stroll through the narrow streets of the city center and explore the many workshops and boutiques dedicated to this traditional craft. Maison HB is a true gem, offering a wide selection of hand-painted Quimper faience items, from plates and bowls to decorative pieces. You can even witness the artisans at work, meticulously painting intricate designs on the pottery.

For a comprehensive overview of Quimper's ceramic heritage, visit the Faience Museum, which houses an impressive collection of historic and contemporary pieces. It's a fantastic opportunity to learn about the craftsmanship and history behind these beautiful ceramics.

In addition to pottery, Quimper boasts a thriving art scene. The Galerie Gloux showcases contemporary art by local artists, while the bustling outdoor market on Place

Copyrighted Material © 210

Saint-Corentin offers a diverse range of arts and crafts, including jewelry, textiles, and paintings. Don't forget to try Kouign-Amann, a delectable Breton pastry, as you explore the town's shopping delights.

Vannes - A Medieval Shopping Paradise

Our journey through Brittany's shopping districts takes us to the captivating city of Vannes. Step back in time as you wander through the well-preserved medieval streets and discover the many charming boutiques tucked away in the city center. Rue Saint-Vincent and Rue du Mené are particularly popular among shoppers, offering a mix of trendy fashion boutiques, artisanal workshops, and unique concept stores.

Art lovers will appreciate the Galerie Art-Tribu, which showcases contemporary works by local and international artists. If

Copyrighted Material © 211

you're in search of authentic Breton fashion, Les P'tits Bouts d'Armor is a boutique that specializes in clothing made from traditional Breton fabrics, such as the iconic striped Breton shirt.

For a taste of Vannes' culinary specialties, visit the Halle aux Poissons, a covered fish market that brims with the freshest seafood caught from the nearby Gulf of Morbihan. Indulge in oysters, mussels, and other delights from the sea. You can also find local delicacies like kouignettes, and bite-sized versions of the famous Kouign-Amann pastry, which make for a perfect treat to enjoy while exploring the city.

Dinan - A Medieval Haven for Antiques

Nestled along the banks of the Rance River, the medieval town of Dinan is a paradise for antique lovers and history enthusiasts. As you stroll through the picturesque streets

Copyrighted Material © 212

lined with half-timbered houses, you'll encounter numerous antique shops and art galleries.

The Rue du Jerzual, a steep and narrow street that leads to the port, is a treasure trove of antique shops. From vintage furniture and collectibles to unique curiosities, you'll find a myriad of treasures waiting to be discovered. Don't miss L'Échoppe, a renowned antique store specializing in furniture and decorative items from various periods.

If you're looking for contemporary art and design, visit the Galerie Artaban. This gallery exhibits a wide range of works by talented local artists, including paintings, sculptures, and ceramics. After browsing the shops, take a moment to soak in the medieval ambiance at one of the charming cafés or tea rooms.

Copyrighted Material © 213

Saint-Malo - A Coastal Shopper's Paradise

Continuing our journey along the captivating coastline of Brittany, we arrive at the historic walled city of Saint-Malo. Known for its maritime heritage and stunning views, Saint-Malo also offers a delightful shopping experience.

Begin your exploration at the bustling Rue Saint Vincent, where you'll find an array of fashion boutiques, jewelry stores, and gift shops. For those seeking nautical-themed treasures, Le Comptoir d'Emile is a must-visit. This charming boutique specializes in maritime-inspired home décor, accessories, and clothing.

As you wander through the cobbled streets, make sure to visit the Saint-Malo Intramuros Market, located in the heart of the fortified city. This vibrant market offers a wide range of local products, including

Copyrighted Material © 214

fresh seafood, artisanal cheeses, and regional specialties like caramel au beurre salé (salted butter caramel). Treat yourself to a box of these delectable caramels to savor later.

Concarneau - A Haven for Art & Craft

Our final stop on this shopping adventure brings us to Concarneau, a picturesque fishing port and a haven for art and craft enthusiasts. Start your exploration at the Ville Close, the fortified old town surrounded by ramparts. Within these historic walls, you'll find an abundance of artisan workshops and galleries.

Art lovers should not miss the Musée de la Pêche, a unique museum dedicated to the history of fishing in Concarneau. Temporary exhibitions featuring the works of regional and international artists are also held at the museum. From paintings and sculptures to

Copyrighted Material © 215

photography and installations, there's always something inspiring to discover.

In the heart of the Ville Close, you'll find La Maison du Cachemire, a boutique that specializes in luxurious cashmere garments and accessories. Treat yourself to a soft and cozy scarf or sweater as a memento of your visit.

Before you leave, make sure to explore the bustling market on Place Jean-Jaurès, where local vendors sell fresh seafood, regional products, and handicrafts. Don't miss the opportunity to taste the famous Concarneau sardines, a local specialty that has been preserved and enjoyed for generations.

A Shopping Journey to Remember

As we conclude our journey through the captivating shopping districts and boutiques of Brittany, we hope you have been inspired

Copyrighted Material © 216

to embark on your adventure. From the medieval charm of Rennes to the faience pottery of Quimper, the historic streets of Vannes, the antique treasures of Dinan, the coastal delights of Saint-Malo, and the art and craft scene of Concarneau, each destination offers a unique shopping experience filled with local specialties and cultural discoveries.

Remember to take your time, immerse yourself in the ambiance, and engage with the friendly locals who are passionate about their craft. Whether you're seeking fashion, art, ceramics, or culinary delights, Brittany's shopping districts and boutiques will leave you with lasting memories and treasures to cherish.

Happy shopping, and may your journey through Brittany be filled with joy, inspiration, and delightful discoveries!

Copyrighted Material © 217

IX. Practical Information

This chapter provides essential practical information to ensure a smooth and enjoyable trip. From transportation and accommodation to communication and safety tips, let's dive into the details of exploring Brittany.

A. Transportation

When planning your trip to Brittany, it's essential to familiarize yourself with the various transportation options available. This guide will provide you with accurate and concise information on getting around by car, public transportation, and the airports and train stations in the region.

Getting Around by Car

Renting a car is a convenient way to explore Brittany and offers the freedom to travel at your own pace. Here are some important things to think about:

★ Rental Services: Several car rental agencies operate in Brittany, both at airports and in major cities. It's advisable to book your car in advance, especially during peak tourist seasons, to ensure availability.

★ Driving License: To rent a car in Brittany, you'll need a valid driver's license from your home country or an International Driving Permit (IDP) if your license is not in English or French. Check with the rental agency for specific requirements.

★ Road Network: Brittany has a well-developed road network, making it relatively easy to navigate. The main highways, known as "autoroutes," connect major cities and towns. Secondary roads, often picturesque, lead to smaller villages and coastal areas.

★ Tolls: Some autoroutes in Brittany have tolls. The fees vary depending on the distance traveled. Make sure to carry sufficient cash or a credit card to pay the tolls. Electronic toll collection systems, such as "Télépéage," are also available for faster payment.

Copyrighted Material © 220

★ Parking: Most towns and cities in Brittany have designated parking areas, both free and paid. Be mindful of parking regulations and restrictions to avoid fines or towing. In popular tourist destinations, it's advisable to arrive early to secure a parking spot.

Public Transportation

Brittany offers a reliable and efficient public transportation system, including buses and trains, which can be an excellent alternative to driving. Here's what you need to know:

★ Buses: The bus network in Brittany is extensive and connects various towns and villages within the region. The buses are cozy and furnished with contemporary conveniences. Tickets can be purchased directly from the driver or at designated ticket offices. Timetables are available online or at bus stops.

Copyrighted Material © 221

★ Trains: The regional train network in Brittany is operated by the French national railway company, SNCF. Trains provide a convenient way to travel between major cities and towns. The main train stations in Brittany include Rennes, Saint-Malo, Brest, Quimper, and Vannes. Train schedules can be accessed online or at the stations.

★ Tickets and Passes: For both buses and trains, you can purchase single tickets for individual trips or consider using passes for more flexibility. The "Carte KorriGo" is a rechargeable card that offers discounted fares and can be used on buses and trains within Brittany.

★ Timeliness: Public transportation in Brittany generally adheres to strict schedules. Buses and trains are known for their punctuality, so it's advisable to arrive at the stations or bus stops a few minutes early to ensure you don't miss your ride.

★ Regional Express Trains (TER): TER trains are a popular option for traveling within Brittany. They provide frequent connections between cities and towns, allowing you to explore different areas of the region easily. Check the TER website or inquire at the train stations for schedules and fares.

Airports & Train Stations

Brittany is well-served by airports and train stations, making it convenient to reach the region and travel within it. Here's what you need to know:

★ Airports: The main airports in Brittany are Rennes Airport (RNS),

Copyrighted Material © 223

Brest Airport (BES), and Lorient South Brittany Airport (LRT). These airports offer domestic and international flights, connecting Brittany with various destinations in Europe. From the airports, you can easily access car rental services, taxis, or public transportation options.

★ Train Stations: Brittany has several major train stations that provide connections to other regions in France and neighboring countries. Rennes is the primary train hub in Brittany, offering high-speed train connections (TGV) to major cities like Paris. Other notable train stations include Saint-Malo, Brest, Quimper, and Vannes.

★ Transportation from Airports and Train Stations: Various transportation options are available to travel from airports and train stations to your desired destination. Taxis are readily available, and you can also use ride-sharing services or pre-booked private transfers. Public transportation, such as buses or regional trains, may also be an option depending on your destination.

★ Facilities and Services: Airports and train stations in Brittany offer a range of amenities, including information desks, luggage storage, currency exchange, and car rental counters. Some larger train stations also have shops, cafes, and waiting lounges for your convenience.

Getting around Brittany is a straightforward and enjoyable experience, thanks to the region's well-connected transportation infrastructure. Whether you choose to explore by car or utilize the public transportation system, you'll have no trouble navigating the beautiful towns,

Copyrighted Material © 225

villages, and coastal areas of Brittany. Remember to plan, check timetables, and make necessary reservations to ensure a smooth and hassle-free journey throughout this enchanting region.

B. Accommodation Options

From luxurious hotels to cozy bed and breakfasts, and self-catering cottages to unique stays, we will provide you with accurate and concise information to help you make an informed decision and create unforgettable memories in Brittany.

Hotels in Brittany

Brittany offers a wide array of hotels, ranging from luxurious five-star establishments to budget-friendly options. Whether you prefer a contemporary boutique hotel or a traditional chateau,

Copyrighted Material © 226

you'll find accommodation that suits your taste.

Luxury Hotels

Experience the epitome of elegance and luxury at Brittany's five-star hotels. These establishments boast opulent amenities, world-class service, and breathtaking views. Indulge in fine dining, relax in luxurious spas, and enjoy personalized concierge services. Some renowned luxury hotels in Brittany include the Château de Locguénolé, Hôtel Barrière Le Royal La Baule, and the Grand Hôtel des Bains in Locquirec.

Boutique Hotels

For those seeking a unique and intimate experience, boutique hotels in Brittany offer a blend of charm and personalized service. These smaller establishments often feature stylish decor, a cozy ambiance, and attention to detail. The Hotel Oceania Brest

Copyrighted Material © 227

Centre and La Maison des Armateurs in Saint-Malo are excellent choices for travelers seeking boutique accommodation.

Budget-Friendly Hotels

If you're traveling on a budget, numerous affordable hotels throughout Brittany offer comfort and convenience. These hotels provide clean and comfortable rooms, basic amenities, and a friendly atmosphere. The Kyriad Prestige Saint-Malo and Hotel Campanile Brest Gouesnou are popular options for budget-conscious travelers.

Bed & Breakfasts in Brittany

For a more personalized and cozy experience, consider staying in a bed and breakfast (B&B) in Brittany. B&Bs offer a warm welcome, a homely ambiance, and a chance to connect with local hosts.

Traditional B&Bs

Copyrighted Material © 228

Brittany is renowned for its traditional stone houses and charming B&Bs. These accommodations provide comfortable rooms, and hearty breakfasts, and often showcase the region's unique architecture. Le Manoir du Hilguy in Paimpol and La Demeure aux Hortensias in Dinan are excellent examples of traditional B&Bs in Brittany.

Farm Stays

Experience the rustic charm of Brittany by choosing a farm stay B&B. These accommodations allow guests to immerse themselves in the region's agricultural heritage and enjoy farm-fresh meals. La Ferme du Vent in Plélan-le-Petit and La Ferme de Balingue in Plouha are popular farm stay options.

Seaside B&Bs

If you're longing for a coastal retreat, Brittany's seaside B&Bs offer stunning views and easy access to the beach. Wake up to the sound of waves crashing and savor a leisurely breakfast overlooking the sea. Le Quai des Princes in Saint-Malo and La Villa des Prés in Perros-Guirec are highly recommended seaside B&Bs.

Self-Catering Cottages in Brittany

For travelers seeking independence and flexibility, self-catering cottages provide a home away from home experience. Brittany's countryside is dotted with charming cottages offering privacy and a chance to explore the region at your own pace.

Coastal Cottages

Brittany's coastline is dotted with picturesque cottages, ideal for those seeking a seaside escape. These cottages often offer breathtaking views, direct beach access, and a tranquil setting. Les Gîtes de Kérisper in Concarneau and Les Maisons de Victoire in Plougrescant are fantastic options for coastal cottage stays.

Rural Retreats

Discover the rustic charm of rural Brittany by choosing a self-catering cottage in the countryside. Surrounded by rolling hills, lush greenery, and quaint villages, these cottages offer a peaceful retreat. Le Moulin du Bois in Malestroit and Le Clos du Moulin in Plogastel-Saint-Germain are perfect choices for a countryside getaway.

Family-Friendly Cottages

Brittany is an excellent destination for family vacations, and there are plenty of self-catering cottages suitable for families. These cottages provide ample space, child-friendly amenities, and outdoor areas

Copyrighted Material © 231

for the little ones to play. La Maison des Lamour in Saint-Briac-sur-Mer and La Maison des Iles in Lannion are highly recommended for families.

Unique Stays in Brittany

For travelers seeking a truly extraordinary experience, Brittany offers a range of unique accommodation options that will leave a lasting impression.

Lighthouses

Stay in a historic lighthouse and enjoy panoramic views of the coastline. Brittany's lighthouse accommodations, such as Phare de Kerbel in Larmor-Plage and Phare de Ploumanac'h in Perros-Guirec, provide a unique opportunity to immerse yourself in maritime history.

Treehouses

Copyrighted Material © 232

Experience the magic of Brittany's forests by staying in a cozy treehouse. These elevated retreats offer a sense of adventure and a chance to reconnect with nature. Les Cabanes du Guern in Plougrescant and Les Cabanes de Kermenguy in Plougonven are popular treehouse accommodations.

Castle Stays

Fulfill your fairytale dreams by staying in a castle in Brittany. These historic properties offer grandeur, luxurious amenities, and a glimpse into the region's medieval past. Château de Kergouanton in Plouézec and Château de Kermezen in Plouguiel are magnificent castle accommodations.

In Brittany, you'll find a plethora of accommodation options to suit every traveler's preferences and budget. Whether you prefer the luxury of hotels, the charm of bed and breakfasts, the independence of self-catering cottages, or the uniqueness of

Copyrighted Material © 233

treehouses and lighthouses, Brittany has it all. Take the time to consider your needs and desires, and use this comprehensive guide to find the perfect accommodation that will enhance your experience in this enchanting region.

C. Communication & Internet Access

Here, we delve into the various communication options and internet access available in Brittany, ensuring you can navigate the region with ease and convenience.

Mobile Communication

Mobile Network Providers

Brittany is well-served by several reliable mobile network providers, offering

Copyrighted Material © 234

extensive coverage across the region. The major providers include Orange, SFR, Bouygues Telecom, and Free Mobile. These operators offer a range of prepaid SIM card options to cater to your specific needs.

Purchasing a SIM Card

To acquire a SIM card, you can visit the network provider's retail stores, and authorized resellers, or purchase them online. Ensure your device is unlocked and compatible with the GSM network (most international phones are). You'll need to present your identification, such as a passport, and provide a local address during registration.

Prepaid Plans

Mobile operators offer prepaid plans that cater to various budgets and requirements. These plans typically include a certain amount of data, voice minutes, and text

Copyrighted Material © 235

messages. Choose a plan that suits your needs, considering factors such as data allowance, validity period, and international calling rates.

Topping Up

Recharging your prepaid SIM card is a straightforward process. You can top up your credit at authorized retail stores, kiosks, supermarkets, or online through the network provider's website or mobile app. Many providers also offer automatic top-up options for added convenience.

Internet Access Options

Wi-Fi Availability

Wi-Fi is readily available in most urban areas of Brittany. Hotels, cafes, restaurants, and public spaces often provide free or paid Wi-Fi services for customers. However, in

Copyrighted Material © 236

more remote or rural areas, the availability of public Wi-Fi may be limited.

Portable Wi-Fi Devices

Consider renting a portable Wi-Fi device, also known as a Mi-Fi or pocket Wi-Fi, which allows you to connect multiple devices simultaneously. These devices can be rented at airports, train stations, or through various online providers. They offer the advantage of constant connectivity, especially when you're on the move or in areas with unreliable or no Wi-Fi coverage.

Internet Cafes

While internet cafes have become less prevalent, you may still find a few in major towns and cities in Brittany. These establishments provide computers with internet access for public use, often charging by the hour. It's advisable to check their operating hours and availability in advance.

Copyrighted Material © 237

Roaming

If you prefer to use your existing mobile plan, check with your home network provider regarding international roaming services and associated costs. While this option provides convenience, it can be expensive, so it's crucial to understand the rates and any data limitations before relying on roaming.

Useful Tips & Considerations

1. Coverage in Rural Areas: While the major towns and cities in Brittany enjoy reliable network coverage, rural areas, particularly in remote coastal regions, may have weaker signals or limited coverage. Plan accordingly and be prepared for intermittent connectivity or consider alternative means of communication in such areas.

Copyrighted Material © 238

2. Emergency Services: In case of emergencies, dial 112 from any mobile or landline phone to reach the emergency services in France. Ensure your mobile phone is charged and has signal reception, especially when traveling in remote areas or engaging in outdoor activities.

3. Messaging and Voice Over IP (VoIP) Apps: To save on international calling and messaging charges, consider using popular messaging apps such as WhatsApp, Skype, or Viber. These apps utilize internet connectivity to facilitate free or low-cost calls, messaging, and even video calls, ensuring you can stay in touch with your loved ones without incurring significant expenses.

4. Language Translation Apps: When traveling to a foreign land, having a

Copyrighted Material © 239

language translation app can be incredibly helpful. Download a reliable translation app like Google Translate, which works offline as well, enabling you to communicate effectively, overcome language barriers, and navigate with ease.

Staying connected while exploring the beautiful region of Brittany is essential for a hassle-free journey. By familiarizing yourself with the available communication options, such as purchasing a local SIM card, utilizing Wi-Fi hotspots, or considering portable Wi-Fi devices, you can ensure seamless connectivity throughout your trip. Remember to plan, consider the coverage in different areas, and leverage modern technologies like messaging apps and translation tools to enhance your experience. Enjoy your time in Brittany, and may your adventures be memorable and well-connected!

Copyrighted Material © 240

D. Useful Phrases & Vocabulary

This comprehensive guidebook aims to equip you with essential phrases and vocabulary to enhance your travel experience in this enchanting region of France. Whether you're exploring the stunning coastline, immersing yourself in rich Celtic culture, or indulging in delectable regional cuisine, mastering these phrases will help you navigate smoothly and connect with the locals. Let's dive in!

Greetings & Basic Expressions:

→ Hello: Bonjour
→ Goodbye: Au revoir
→ Thank you: Merci
→ You're welcome: De rien
→ Excuse me: Excusez-moi
→ Please: S'il vous plaît
→ Yes: Oui
→ No: Non
→ I'm sorry: Je suis désolé(e)

→ How are you?: Comment ça va?

Getting Around:

→ Where is...?: Où est...?
→ Can you help me, please?: Pouvez-vous m'aider, s'il vous plaît?
→ How much is the ticket?: Combien coûte le billet?
→ Train station: Gare
→ Bus station: Gare routière
→ Airport: Aéroport
→ Taxi: Taxi
→ Left: Gauche
→ Right: Droite
→ Straight ahead: Tout droit

Accommodation:

→ Hotel: Hôtel
→ Room: Chambre
→ Reservation: Réservation
→ Check-in: Enregistrement
→ Check-out: Départ

Copyrighted Material © 242

→ Do you have any available rooms?: Avez-vous des chambres disponibles?

→ Is breakfast included?: Le petit-déjeuner est-il compris?

→ Can I have the Wi-Fi password?: Puis-je avoir le mot de passe Wi-Fi?

→ Where's the nearest ATM?: Où se trouve le distributeur le plus proche?

→ Can I have a wake-up call, please?: Puis-je avoir un réveil, s'il vous plaît?

Dining Out:

→ Table for two, please: Une table pour deux, s'il vous plaît

→ Menu: Menu

→ Water: Eau

→ Wine: Vin

→ Starter: Entrée

→ Main course: Plat principal

→ Dessert: Dessert

→ Bill, please: L'addition, s'il vous plaît

Copyrighted Material © 243

→ Do you have any vegetarian options?:Avez-vous des options végétariennes?

→ I'm allergic to...: Je suis allergique à...

Exploring & Sightseeing:

→ What are the must-see attractions?: Quelles sont les attractions incontournables?

→ Can you recommend a good restaurant?: Pouvez-vous recommander un bon restaurant?

→ Where's the nearest beach?: Où se trouve la plage la plus proche?

→ Could you take a photo of us, please?: Pourriez-vous nous prendre en photo, s'il vous plaît?

→ What time does it open/close?: À quelle heure ça ouvre/ferme?

→ Is there a guided tour available?: Y a-t-il une visite guidée disponible?

→ Is it far from here?: Est-ce loin d'ici?

Copyrighted Material © 244

→ Can you show it on the map?: Pouvez-vous le montrer sur la carte?

→ I'm interested in local history: Je suis intéressé(e) par l'histoire locale.

→ Are there any festivals happening?: Y a-t-il des festivals en cours?

Emergencies:

→ Help!: Au secours!

→ I need a doctor: J'ai besoin d'un médecin

→ Where's the nearest pharmacy?: Où se trouve la pharmacie la plus proche?

→ Call the police: Appelez la police

→ I lost my passport: J'ai perdu mon passeport

→ Can you recommend a reliable locksmith?: Pouvez-vous recommander un serrurier fiable?

→ I had an accident: J'ai eu un accident

→ Fire: Incendie

→ I've been robbed: On m'a volé

Copyrighted Material © 245

→ I don't feel well: Je ne me sens pas bien

Congratulations! With these useful phrases and vocabulary at your disposal, you're ready to embark on an unforgettable journey through Brittany. Immerse yourself in the local culture, engage in meaningful conversations, and make lifelong memories. Remember, even a basic attempt to speak the local language will be appreciated by the warm and welcoming people of Brittany. Bon voyage!

E. Itineraries

This wonderful guide also aims to provide you with a curated selection of itineraries, ensuring that you make the most of your time in this captivating destination. From the rugged coastline and charming medieval towns to the mystical forests and world-renowned cuisine, Brittany promises to enchant and inspire you at every turn. So, let us dive into the depths of this captivating region and unveil the hidden treasures it holds.

Itinerary 1: Coastal Splendor

Day 1: Arrival in Rennes & the Charm of Dinard (Distance: 73 km)

Begin your adventure in Rennes, the capital city of Brittany. Immerse yourself in the medieval charm of its historic center, explore the Parliament of Brittany, and stroll along the charming cobblestone streets.

Afterward, make your way to Dinard, a picturesque coastal town known for its Belle Époque architecture and stunning beaches. Enjoy a stroll along the Promenade du Clair de Lune, offering breathtaking views of the English Channel.

Copyrighted Material © 247

*Day 2: Exploring the Emerald Coast
(Distance: 69 km)*

Venture along the Emerald Coast, starting with a visit to Saint-Malo. Wander through the imposing walls of this fortified city, visit the St. Vincent Cathedral, and indulge in delectable seafood at one of the local restaurants.

Continue your journey to Cancale, a charming fishing village celebrated for its oysters. Savor the freshest seafood while overlooking the beautiful bay.

Conclude your day with a visit to the mystical abbey of Mont Saint-Michel, an architectural marvel rising from the sea. Explore the narrow streets, ascend to the abbey's pinnacle, and witness the mesmerizing tides that surround this UNESCO World Heritage site.

Itinerary 2: Medieval Marvels

Copyrighted Material © 248

Day 1: Quaint Streets of Vannes (Distance: 108km)

Begin your exploration in Vannes, a city teeming with medieval history. Discover the well-preserved ramparts, visit the magnificent Cathedral of Saint Peter, and lose yourself in the charming alleys of the historic center.

Don't miss the opportunity to cruise along the Gulf of Morbihan, a mesmerizing bay dotted with numerous islands. Marvel at the natural beauty and abundant birdlife that call this place home.

Day 2: Mystical Forests & Historic Treasures (Distance: 100km)

Head to the mystical Brocéliande Forest shrouded in legends of King Arthur and the Knights of the Round Table. Explore the enchanting trails, visit the iconic Fountain

Copyrighted Material © 249

of Youth, and seek the mythical Merlin's Tomb.

Continue your journey to Josselin, a town renowned for its medieval castle overlooking the Nantes-Brest Canal. Marvel at its striking architecture, visit the Basilica of Notre-Dame-du-Roncier and stroll along the canal's tranquil banks.

Itinerary 3: Cultural Delights

Day 1: Nantes & Artistic Marvels (Distance: 110km)

Begin your cultural exploration in Nantes, a city that seamlessly blends history with modernity. Visit the impressive Château des Ducs de Bretagne, delve into the creative world of the Machines de l'Île, and admire the contemporary artwork at the Musée d'Arts de Nantes.

Copyrighted Material © 250

Take a stroll along the scenic banks of the River Erdre, lined with elegant 19th-century mansions and picturesque landscapes.

Day 2: Carnac & Quimper (Distance: 208km)

Discover the mysterious alignments of Carnac, a megalithic site shrouded in ancient history. Witness thousands of standing stones and explore the fascinating Carnac Museum, unraveling the secrets of this enigmatic place.

Conclude your journey in Quimper, a town renowned for its rich Celtic heritage and beautiful medieval architecture. Visit the impressive Quimper Cathedral, wander through the charming Old Town, and admire the exquisite Faience pottery.

Dear travelers, Brittany invites you to unlock its wonders and immerse yourself in its captivating beauty. Whether you choose

Copyrighted Material © 251

to traverse the breathtaking coastline, explore medieval marvels, or indulge in cultural delights, this region promises an unforgettable experience. From the moment you set foot in Brittany, you will be entranced by its history, bewitched by its landscapes, and enchanted by its culture. So, pack your bags, embrace the allure of Brittany, and embark on a journey that will leave an indelible mark on your heart and soul. Bon voyage!

Copyrighted Material © 252

X. Additional Resources

Whether you're planning a relaxing beach vacation or a journey through ancient castles, this part of this guide will provide you with all the necessary information to make your trip to Brittany an unforgettable experience. Here in this chapter, we will explore various online resources, tourist information centers, as well as maps, and navigation apps that will assist you in navigating the region and discovering its hidden gems. Let's embark on this journey together!

A. Online Resources

Official Tourism Websites

The official tourism websites for Brittany and its major cities, such as Rennes, Saint-Malo, and Quimper, are excellent starting points for planning your trip. These websites offer comprehensive information on attractions, accommodations, transportation, events, and more. They often provide interactive maps, suggested itineraries, and useful tips to enhance your travel experience.

Travel Forums & Blogs

Joining online travel forums and reading travel blogs can provide valuable insights from fellow travelers who have visited Brittany. Websites like TripAdvisor, Lonely Planet's Thorn Tree, and Reddit's r/travel are popular platforms where you can ask questions, seek advice, and gain firsthand knowledge from experienced travelers.

Social Media Platforms

Follow official tourism accounts on platforms like Instagram, Facebook, and Twitter to stay updated on the latest events, festivals, and attractions in Brittany. Additionally, hashtags such as #VisitBrittany or #ExploreBrittany can help you discover hidden gems and connect with other travelers sharing their experiences.

Mobile Apps

Several mobile apps are designed specifically to assist travelers in Brittany. From comprehensive travel guides to offline maps and language translation, these apps can be invaluable during your trip. Some recommended apps include "Brittany Travel Guide and Offline Map," "Google Maps," "Duolingo" for language learning, and "XE Currency" for currency conversion.

B. Tourist Information Centers

Regional Tourist Offices

Brittany has an extensive network of regional tourist offices that offer a wealth of information, brochures, and assistance to visitors. These offices are usually located in major cities and popular tourist destinations. Knowledgeable staff members can guide attractions, transportation, accommodations, and local events. They may also offer city maps, public transportation schedules, and discounted tickets to attractions.

Local Tourist Offices

In addition to regional tourist offices, many towns and smaller communities in Brittany have their own local tourist offices. These offices are especially helpful for exploring off-the-beaten-path destinations and discovering authentic local experiences. The staff can provide information on local festivals, markets, hiking trails, and

Copyrighted Material © 256

lesser-known attractions that may not be prominently featured in mainstream travel guides.

Tourist Information Centers at Airports & Train Stations

If you're arriving in Brittany by air or train, make sure to visit the tourist information centers located at major airports and train stations. These centers can provide you with maps, brochures, and detailed transportation information tailored to your arrival point. They can also assist with booking accommodations, arranging transportation, and answering any specific queries you may have about your journey.

C. Maps & Navigation Apps

Paper Maps

Having a physical map of Brittany is always a good idea, especially if you prefer a tangible reference. You can obtain detailed maps from tourist information centers, and bookstores, or order them online in advance. Paper maps are particularly useful for planning your route, understanding the geography of the region, and exploring areas with limited internet connectivity.

Online Maps

Digital maps are a convenient and reliable tool for navigating Brittany. Google Maps is widely used and trusted for its comprehensive coverage and accurate directions. It offers detailed street maps, satellite imagery, and real-time traffic updates. You can use Google Maps to plan routes, find nearby attractions, locate restaurants and accommodations, and even explore public transportation options. Make sure to download the offline maps of

Copyrighted Material © 258

Brittany to access them without an internet connection.

GPS Navigation Apps

In addition to Google Maps, several GPS navigation apps are specifically tailored for travelers. These apps provide turn-by-turn navigation, voice guidance, and real-time traffic information. Some popular options include Waze, Sygic, and Maps.me. These apps can help you navigate through Brittany's winding roads, find parking spaces, and avoid congestion.

Brittany-Specific Apps

There are also apps designed specifically for exploring Brittany. For example, the "Brittany Ferries" app provides ferry schedules, reservations, and onboard services. The "BreizhGo" app offers information on public transportation in the region, including bus and train schedules.

Copyrighted Material © 259

These apps can be particularly useful if you plan to travel within Brittany using public transportation or ferries.

Congratulations! You are now equipped with a wealth of resources to make your trip to Brittany a remarkable adventure. By utilizing the online resources mentioned in this guide, such as official tourism websites, travel forums, and social media platforms, you can gather valuable information and insider tips. The tourist information centers, both regional and local, will provide personalized assistance and recommendations, ensuring you don't miss out on the hidden treasures of the region. Finally, maps and navigation apps, including Google Maps, GPS navigation apps, and Brittany-specific apps, will guide you seamlessly through the beautiful landscapes and charming towns of Brittany.

Copyrighted Material © 260

XI. Conclusion

As we come to the end of this comprehensive Brittany travel guide, it's time to provide you with some final tips and recommendations to make your journey through this beautiful region even more memorable.

A. Final Tips & Recommendations

Here are some key insights to enhance your travel experience:

★ Embrace the Coastal Beauty: Brittany boasts an enchanting coastline that stretches for miles, offering breathtaking views and pristine beaches. Don't miss the opportunity to explore the stunning Pink Granite

Copyrighted Material © 261

Coast, with its unique rock formations and crystal-clear waters. Take leisurely walks along the coastal paths, bask in the sun on sandy beaches, and indulge in water sports like kayaking, sailing, and surfing.

★ Explore the Historical Sites: Brittany's rich history is evident in its ancient towns and well-preserved castles. Visit the historic walled city of Saint-Malo, where you can wander through its narrow streets and admire the impressive fortifications. Explore the medieval town of Dinan, with its half-timbered houses and charming cobblestone streets. Don't forget to tour the majestic Mont Saint-Michel, an architectural wonder rising from the sea.

★ Immerse Yourself in Celtic Culture: Brittany has a strong Celtic heritage, and you can experience its vibrant

Copyrighted Material © 262

culture through traditional music, dance, and festivals. Attend a Breton music concert or a fest-noz (night festival) to witness locals showcasing their traditional dance moves. Visit the Museum of Breton Culture in Quimper to delve deeper into the region's Celtic roots.

★ Sample the Gastronomic Delights: Brittany is renowned for its delectable seafood, and you simply can't leave without savoring some of its culinary delights. Indulge in fresh oysters, succulent lobster, and mouthwatering crepes, which are a specialty of the region. Visit the charming fishing villages along the coast to enjoy authentic seafood platters and discover local markets for farm-fresh produce.

★ Get Off the Beaten Path: While popular tourist destinations in

Brittany are undoubtedly worth exploring, consider venturing off the beaten path to discover hidden gems. Head to the rugged landscapes of the Crozon Peninsula or the picturesque village of Locronan. Take a boat trip to the Îles de Glénan, a group of stunning islands known for their turquoise waters and white sand beaches.

★ Respect the Environment: As responsible travelers, it is important to respect and preserve the natural beauty of Brittany. Follow designated trails, avoid littering, and be mindful of fragile ecosystems. Support local initiatives and eco-friendly practices, such as using reusable water bottles and opting for sustainable transportation options whenever possible.

Copyrighted Material © 264

B. Fond Farewell to Brittany

As we bid adieu to Brittany, we hope that this travel guide has equipped you with all the necessary information and inspiration for an unforgettable journey. Whether you choose to explore the picturesque coastal towns, delve into the region's rich history, or simply relax amidst breathtaking natural beauty, Brittany offers a truly captivating experience.

Remember to immerse yourself in the local culture, savor the delectable gastronomy, and embark on adventures that will create lasting memories. The charm and authenticity of Brittany lie in its diverse landscapes, warm-hearted locals, and its ability to transport you to a world of timeless beauty.

As an experienced traveler, I encourage you to approach your travels in Brittany with an open mind and a willingness to embrace new experiences. Let the region's enchanting scenery and fascinating history captivate you. Take the time to connect with the locals, who are known for their hospitality and love for their homeland.

May your journey through Brittany be filled with joy, discovery, and a profound appreciation for the wonders of this remarkable region. Farewell for now, and bon voyage!

Copyrighted Material © 266

HAPPY BRITTANY TRAVELS!

Copyrighted Material © 267

Printed in Great Britain
by Amazon

25211528R00149